Christian Ethics in the Protestant Tradition

Waldo Beach

John Knox Press
ATLANTA

Library of Congress Cataloging-in-Publication Data

Beach, Waldo.
    Christian ethics in the Protestant tradition / Waldo Beach.
      p. cm.
    Bibliography: p.
    Includes index.
    ISBN 0-8042-0793-3 (pbk.) :
      1. Christian ethics.   I. Title.
BJ1251.B366 1988
241'.0404—dc19

88-8213
CIP

© copyright John Knox Press 1988
10 9 8 7 6 5 4 3 2 1
Printed in the United States of America
John Knox Press
Atlanta, Georgia 30365

Preface

In recent years many valuable new texts have been published on Christian ethics and moral theology from the Roman Catholic perspective. There have not been, however, a comparable number representing the Protestant tradition. This introductory text is intended to fill this gap. Written primarily for use at the seminary level it may also prove of value for upper-class undergraduate courses in departments of religion, as well as for the general reader concerned about the moral quandaries of our time and the wisdom that Christian ethics may bring to bear on them.

As an introductory text, it attempts to survey in cursory fashion the theological premises, the Christian moral norms, and their application to the ethical dilemmas both of private life and public policy. It is pitched somewhere between the formidable tomes of moral theology on the one hand and the quick-fix manuals for Christian living on the other. For each chapter there is a suggested bibliography that may be used to explore in depth the problems of the issues raised.

A special word of appreciation is in order to those who have offered valuable critical suggestions both as to the book's style and substance: Professor Walter Benjamin, Professor Stanley Hauerwas, Sister Evelyn Mattern of the North Carolina Council of Churches, and Mrs. Nancy Fulcher. My chief indebtedness is to the generations of students whom I have taught in the Divinity School and the graduate school at Duke University, with whom it has been a constant inspiration to explore these issues in classroom discussion.

Waldo Beach
Durham, North Carolina

Contents

PART I
Principles of Christian Ethics

1

The Challenge of Secular Culture to Christian Ethics

How should an introductory text on Christian ethics begin? Should it start from square one, from scratch, to inform a blank mind, as one might start to learn Russian or physics? Or is it more plausible to assume that since we live in a culture that is more or less Christian in its history and traditions, we already know in general what Christian ethics is? The problem is only to remind us of our tradition and then to show the ways we should practice the moral standards we accept in theory. If the latter, since there are so many disparate voices claiming to speak for the truly Christian way, which brand of Christian ethics is the true one and, conversely, which one is false? We are immediately into a quagmire.

One preliminary matter in this mire must be clarified, if possible, before a systematic construction of Christian ethical theory can be addressed. Can we affirm whether the operating moral premises of our culture are Christian or secular?

Three Meanings of *Secular*

Much hangs on the meaning of the word *secular*, and what might be defined as the process of secularization. In the strict and narrow sense of the word, of course, *secular* comes from the Latin *saeculum*, meaning "this age," or "this world." The process of secularization in its first and simplest sense means the embodiment of religious ideals and norms into the culture of the world. Let us call this Secularization I. The transcendent "Word became flesh and dwelt among us" (John 1:14). This is the embodiment of the divine into the human. One may point to instances in history again and again of Secularization I. In the Roman Empire, the Christian moral ideal of fidelity in love set the monogamous family pattern as normative. In the Reformation of the sixteenth century, Martin Luther's ideal of "vocation" and the "priesthood of all believers" gave to common secular work a sacred worth and radically changed the motives and patterns of the economy. In the seventeenth century, the Puritans in Massachusetts Bay set up a God-governed "holy commonwealth," whose political structure expressed the Christian ideal of God's rule over the body politic, a theocracy. In the twentieth century, the inspiration of the Christian norm of human worth and the equality of all persons inspired the civil rights movement, as earlier in the nineteenth century the abolitionist movement, inspired by the Christian conscience of the churches, fought against slavery. All these represent a translation of sacred ideals, inspired by a vision of a divine transcendent order, into structural and systemic changes in the social order. The sacred transforms the secular as persons act in obedience to the petition "Thy kingdom come, . . . On earth as it is in heaven."

The second meaning of secularization (call it Secularization II) is of the opposite kind. This process of secularization is one in which the various spheres of human activity are freed from any theological, transcendent frame of reference or church control. Each becomes a kind of law unto itself, playing its game by its own rules. No longer is there a single "sacred canopy," to use Peter Berger's phrase, covering the government, the economy, the home, the school, the arts. Harvey Cox defined this kind of secularization as "the disappearance of religious determination of the symbols of cultural integration."[1] In this sense, politics is politics, subject to no moral law higher than the shrewd ways of gaining and keeping power. Economics is no longer that sector of morality, under the control of the medieval church, dealing with the ways the physical resources of the earth should be produced and consumed for the common good under a higher law. Economics now is a law to itself. Education, science, the family, the arts, likewise are secularized, accountable to no transcendent norm or authority, church or otherwise. In the realm of education, for instance, though some mottos and inscriptions are sung in the alma mater and some of the architecture of the early buildings links wisdom to piety, current educational practice is entirely functional, pragmatic, and devoid of a sacred halo. The lab session for chemistry 202 does not open or close with prayer. That is why in a typical American college or university the courses bear no integral relation to each other. The university is a multiversity.

A third interpretation of the meaning of *secular* is in a sense the end result of Secularization II. Secularism itself becomes a religion. In our conventional way of thinking, *secular* means "nonreligious" or "irreligious" or "opposed to religion." Although it may upset conventional wisdom, if we use the term *religion* in the broadest and most inclusive sense (meaning the faith-system on which a person relies to give significance to his or her life), then we may say that our culture is a devoutly "religious" one. The term *religion* is used here in the sense Paul Tillich meant when he spoke of "object of ultimate concern." In this sense, there are many "gods" in our so-called secular culture, the objects of loyalty and trust and devotion. These are gods in the sense Martin Luther meant when he wrote, "Whatever your heart relies upon. . .is properly speaking your god." This presumes a certain view of human nature: we are creatures who are animals that must have food and sleep, yes, but we are more than animals. We are spiritual beings, creatures with minds and hearts who require some "center of value" ultimately treasured, whatever that may be, on which we count to sustain us and to which we try to be faithful. In this loose sense of the word *secular*, we cannot be human and not be religious.

4

PRINCIPLES OF CHRISTIAN ETHICS

The Secular Gods of American Culture

If we follow this third definition of secularization (call it Secularization III, if you like) it becomes readily apparent that many gods are worshiped in twentieth-century America. Some may seem rather small demigods—consider, for example, the fervor with which some Bostonians worship the Celtics or some Texans adore the Dallas Cowboys, treating their victories or defeats as life-and-death matters. But most of the secular religions in the practicing polytheism of our culture are of larger dimension. I discuss three in this section. Incidentally, each has its own "systematic theology," not in the sense used in theology textbooks, but as the syndrome of their basic premises.

The following are the cardinal beliefs, hidden or explicit, to be found in our major secular religions:

- the method of truth seeking: epistemology
- the nature of ultimate reality: ontology or metaphysics
- the nature of human nature: anthropology
- the agency or power that can save human beings from problems and predicaments: soteriology
- the direction and anticipated end of human history: eschatology

Whether or not we use the formal, technical terms, these faith-premises underlie and validate in each religion the distinctive ethical norms that those who hold these faiths are expected to follow.

The first of the dominant faiths is *scientism*. Equipped with all the high technology of radar, microchips, computers, space shuttles, this faith is converting millions daily in its laboratory temples. In the religion of scientism, the realm of mystery that people in earlier eras approached with awe and reverence is now approached with curiosity. By the use of the inductive method, the mysterious is explained away and the awesome is desacralized. For the Christian, knowledge begins and ends in wonder and reverence. For one of scientific faith, initial wonder moves through curiosity and ends in explanation, which is then put to use in technology. As legend has it, Isaac Newton was sitting under a tree. An apple fell on his head. He did not then kneel in prayer.

Rather, he asked, "How come?" He then proposed the hypothesis of the law of gravity, a hypothesis confirmed by other natural events. On that basis the principle of gravity is used to manipulate the things of nature for the machineries of human convenience.

In the anthropology of the religion of scientism, we human beings share with our simian ancestry many animal traits, but we are also distinctive in our powers of reason, our ingenuity in using tools to manipulate our environment. We are so ingenious that we can propel ourselves to the moon or orbit the earth in outer space and send pictures by satellite to the folks watching on TV at home. Our ingenuity in splitting the atom gives us new sources of energy for heat and light, although it also enables us to develop atomic weapons that might lead to human genocide.

To be sure, the human situation is not completely a blessed one. There are all kinds of maladjustments—persons with each other, states with states, nations with nations, and humanity with the natural environment. But for one who trusts in science, these maladjustments can be remedied, not by prayer or a rain dance or a sacrifice laid on the ancient altars, but by applying the scientific method to the problem at hand. Scientific technique is savior. So the classical Christian scenario of sin and salvation is replaced by a new soteriology: problem-solution. The faith of the scientist, from physicist to psychologist, is that the application of scientific skills will lead progressively from a primitive prescientific culture to a utopia, an air-conditioned heaven on earth. This is the eschatology of scientism.

The second of the secular religions of our culture is capitalism. Its theology is more diffuse, perhaps, than the religion of scientism, but its influence on the hearts and minds of its devotees is no less pervasive. In a strict and narrow sense, capitalism means an economic system in which the production, distribution, and consumption of goods are carried on by private enterprise under competitive conditions. In a broader sense, capitalism becomes a kind of religion in which this mode of economic transaction is trusted as of ultimate significance and worth.[2] All aspects of human experience are read in economic terms and translated into the cost-benefit equation. Truth value equals cash value. Certain fixed principles of human transaction have an almost metaphysical status: the law of supply and demand, a favorable balance of trade, and free enterprise, which assumes that human welfare depends on unregulated economic activity. This individualism does not go against the common good, it is claimed, for according to Adam Smith, the "theologian" of the capitalistic faith, if each person works for himself or herself, the "Unseen Hand" ensures the corporate good.

Human beings are by nature acquisitive animals, who seek above all economic security for ourselves and our families and who find self-realization or "salvation" in excelling in the competitive market. The courtesies of etiquette inherited from the Christian tradition are now practiced as self-promotional devices. "May I help you?" really means "Can I sell you something?" Yes, there are such problems as chronic unemployment, the huge federal budget deficit, the ecological destruction caused by uncontrolled growth, the depersonalization of industrial urbanization, but all these can be solved by an arrangement of resources, energy, and human labor that achieves maximum productivity and maximum profit. The index of human well-being is the growth line of the GNP. The good consists in goods. The quantity of things one possesses is the measure of the quality of one's life.

The third hidden religion in American culture is what is commonly called civil religion,[3] or "Americanity." The object of ultimate trust and devotion is the nation. The involved historical story of the relation of the Christian faith to American political theory need not detain us here. In earlier eras, the foundation of our government was clearly a Christian one. The "civil religion" of the Founding Fathers was a theistic faith, as a close reading of this period confirms. In our own day, civil religion has come to mean the secularization of American democracy, the worship of America as "the land of the free and the home of the brave." We are God's "chosen people." Self-realization lies in patriotic devotion to our country in time of war or peace. Our mission is to combat the demonic powers of godless communism and to spread the benefits of democracy across the world. That is our "manifest destiny."

These three secular faiths—scientism, capitalism, and Americanity—fit rather neatly with each other. They are not warring gods; they join in a kind of synthetic faith. The ends of capitalism are furthered by scientific technique and enterprise, and the multinational corporations centered in the United States further our national self-interest abroad and bring us prosperity at home.

The Secularization of Christian Churches

It is readily apparent also that these secular religions have profoundly influenced the institutions that presumably are the vital centers of the Christian faith, namely, the Christian churches. If one asks whether the traffic of influence flows more strongly from Christian churches to secular culture or from secular culture to the churches, it is plain that the secular deities of common culture influence the church far more than the God of the Christian faith influences the culture. Efficiency more than godliness is the criterion by which the pastor's success in a church is measured. Budget rather than vision determines policy. In many electronic churches of the conservative evangelical sort, high technology is used shrewdly, and skills in making money are practiced in the name of Christ, even under the sign of the cross. Civil religion, as well, practically identifies Christianity with American democracy. "This nation under God" is taken to mean that the God of the Christian faith is a kind of honorary president, *ex officio*, and that national self-interest is part of the divine plan.

If this quick analysis of the dynamics of contemporary American culture is at all accurate, we are led to conclude that, despite our bland assumption that Christianity is the informally established religion of America, authentic Christianity is in fact a minority movement. Although we might like to hold a fond illusion that the church is in the world, converting the world from secularism to Christianity, the fact is that the world is in the church, converting the church to secularism. The preceding analysis now makes it difficult but all the more necessary to attempt to define authentic Christianity, as opposed to its counterfeits, and to articulate its faith-premises and its ethical norms.

2

The Field
of Christian
Ethics

What *is* ethics, anyway? Dictionary definitions are abstract. They do not lead us much beyond "the discipline that articulates the moral standards that constitute the good life" or "the criteria by which persons determine what they ought to be and do" or "the systematic analysis of those habits of behavior which constitute virtues or misbehavior which constitute vices." Ethics is not all of one kind by any means. There are obviously many schools of ethical thought and diverse traditions: Stoic, Epicurean, utilitarian, Kantian, Marxian, positivistic. The subject of this book, *Christian* ethics, is but one of many ways of ethical reflection. Its distinctive character is determined by the theological premises of the Christian faith, on which it is based.

Delineating Christian ethics by locating it as though on a map may help. It is a discipline of reflection and analysis that lies between Christian theology on one side and social sciences on the other or, to put it in shorthand, between the faith and the facts.

From Christian theology, it derives the faith-premises that validate its moral norms. From the sciences that study human behavior, it derives the understanding of the complex factors in the psychology of human nature and the cultural circumstances surrounding the problems of choice and decision. It is imperative that Christian ethics pay close attention to its neighbor disciplines on both sides. When Christian ethics, in theory or practice, is concerned only with the theological premises and is blind to the factual data that the sociologist, the economist, the psychologist, the political scientist, or just everyday experience may provide, Christian ethics becomes moralistic, unrealistic, and irrelevant to the problems in decisions that persons must make. If, on the other hand, Christian ethical reflection and decision are based solely on the data of social science, with no attention to the Christian tradition, then choices in action become unprincipled, normless, anomic.

Here we encounter the old "is-ought" problem. What is called the naturalistic fallacy is the flaw of believing that the moral "ought" is derived only from the empirical "is." That is a perilous route. A Gallup poll of how people *do* behave is not the sole criterion for deciding how they *ought* to behave. Authentic morality is not determined by majority vote. If a majority of students in an inner-city high school are hooked on hard drugs, do we then conclude that they ought to be? No. If the dominant power elite in South Africa have imposed apartheid, does that mean it is morally right? No, you cannot derive a moral "ought" from an empirical "is." True morals are not just a compendium of mores. The "desired" does not itself constitute the "desirable." For Judeo-Christian ethics the moral "ought" comes from the other side: what the theological faith-premises affirm about the transcendent will of God, however that may be understood.

But the voice of realism reminds us that as we are accountable ultimately to what the divine will requires, we are also accountable to the hard facts that set the limits of possible choice. Ethical decisions must make their careful, deliberate way between what is ideal and what is possible under the circumstances.

Although there are many styles and schools of ethical theory, all schools of *philosophical* ethics rest on certain bottom-line premises about the nature of ultimate reality. This is called meta-ethics. Although Christian morality includes many differing persuasions and traditions, all have beneath them certain theological premises and foundations.

Is Christian ethics then only a family name shared by persons of quite different moral persuasions? Certainly on any one debate about right and wrong in current policy and practice, such as homosexuality, abortion, economic policies, or national defense, we do not hear a unanimous voice from the Christian communities. Quite the contrary. Citing some major typologies of ethical theory may help to explain these differences.[1]

Main Types of Ethical Theory

One long-established distinction is that between teleological and deontological ethics. Teleological ethics asks first: what is the great goal or end (*telos*) of human striving? When that question is answered, ethics then becomes the discipline that spells out the means or steps by which that goal can be realized or approached. This might be called the ethics of the *good*, the ethics of aspiration. Deontological ethics, on the other hand, asks: *what* or *who* is the supreme authority, setting the commands or laws by which one ought to live? It is the ethics of the *right*, the ethics of obedience and obligation.

In the history of Christian ethics through twenty centuries, many examples of deontological and teleological ethics can be found. Roman Catholic ethics of the scholastic type, for instance, based on Aristotle's teleological ethics of striving for *eudaimonia* (or "well-being"), translated that *telos* into the *viseo Dei*, the vision of God, to be attained by the diligent cultivation of good habits of the virtues, which lead one toward the beatific vision. Another example is the Protestant ethics of the Social Gospel movement, whose goal is the kingdom of God on earth, toward which we will progress by systemic changes in the economic order.

On the other hand, examples of deontological ethics are to be found in Roman Catholic form in the papal encyclicals, which lay down the law for the faithful on the ethics of divorce or contraception, or in Protestant versions that take the commands of God as found in the Bible to be absolute. The Bible becomes a rule book, and the Christian life consists in obeying the specific letters of its laws.

Incidentally, two similar outer actions may be taken from a deontological motive or a teleological motive. A Christian pacifist may take a stand against the military policy of the government simply out of obedience to the biblical commandment "Thou shalt not kill"; another Christian pacifist may take the same stance in hopes that the peace rally he or she is organizing may be but one step toward realizing the future high goal of a peaceable kingdom on earth, a warless world.

As a matter of fact, the distinction between the ethics of obligation and the ethics of aspiration, however useful, need not connote two separate bins into which all ethicists can be sorted. There may be crossovers and mixtures of motives. As H. Richard Niebuhr has suggested in his *Responsible Self*,[2] the model of the ethics of "response," the ethics of the fitting, transcends and incorporates both types. The ethics of response and responsibility does not start with the question, what is the great goal of human striving? Nor with the question, what is the supreme law of all? It starts rather with the question, how is the divine will acting in this present time? And then, how shall our action respond in a manner fitting to the divine action?

Roman Catholic and Protestant Ethics

Another way of explaining the difference among types of Christian ethics is to distinguish the main *historic* church traditions. If we extend the term *Christian* to mean "Judeo-Christian," we have of course three main traditions: Jewish, Roman Catholic, and Protestant. One could not possibly understand the ethics of the early Christian church without understanding the Judaic roots from which it sprang, and insofar as Protestantism centers on the Bible as authoritative for morality, plainly the Jewish tradition of the Old Testament is normative. For the purposes of this book, I omit the consideration of the ethics of Judaism as a separate type, considering instead the points of convergence and divergence between Roman Catholic and Protestant ethical theory.[3]

As already noted, Roman Catholic ethical theory, all the way from Thomas Aquinas in the thirteenth century to the American Council of Bishops' Pastoral Letters on war and peace and the economy, has been mainly teleological in style, but with some deontological elements in the treatment of laws. Thomas Aquinas, the official "theologian" of the Roman church, has set the definitive pattern of the church's theology and ethics. In the great hierarchy of God's kingdom, human beings, created between angels and animals, are endowed with the gifts of reason and free will, which enable us to make rational choices. We also are endowed with a natural capacity to distinguish right from wrong, which when properly schooled by reason can be called the conscience, the capacity to apply universal principles to practical choices. When guided by reason and conscience, persons cultivate the internal habits of the seven virtues: the four cardinal virtues of temperance, courage, justice, and prudence, inherited from Greek philosophy, to which are added the three theological virtues of faith, hope, and love. The Creator also sets for humanity external guidelines that lead to moral perfection: the structure of laws. "Eternal law" is the transcendent blueprint of the whole order of the universe in the mind of the Creator. "Natural law" is the enactment of God's eternal law in the created world and discerned by human reason. A first principle of natural law is that good is to be sought and evil avoided. Other examples of natural law principles are the right of self-preservation, private property for common use, the rights of parents to procreate and nurture their children in true faith. Human laws, or positive laws, are good insofar as they are in accord with the principles of natural law, bad if they are not. There is also "divine law," the special revealed laws of God in the Bible. When human beings cultivate the virtues of the Christian life and follow the precepts of natural law, we are on the road to eternal blessedness. But of course we often falter or wander from that high road. God's grace as present in Christ in the church he established becomes an instrument of grace through the ministry of sacraments, to forgive human sin and to set human beings back on the path to eternal blessedness. Though the virtues of the good life and the principles of natural law can be known and observed by all persons, the special grace of God is the province of the church's authority. True salvation, therefore, cannot be realized outside the Roman church.

The Protestant Reformation got its main inspiration from the career of a young, brilliant, devout monk, Martin Luther, who early in the sixteenth century, as he studied and taught Scripture, came to question more and more this teleological ethic and the basic notion that the Christian earns entrance to heaven by the works of righteousness. Luther became persuaded, as St. Paul had expressed it in the letter to the Romans, that the Christian life is not a school of moral gymnastics. Entrance to heaven is not based on earning a high ethical GPA. No, we are saved by no merits of our own but solely by the grace of God revealed in Christ. *Sola fide.* "Justification by grace through faith alone."

The Roman church of Luther's day was in a period of decline and decay. Its power in Europe led to many corrupt practices by which believers were promised that they could purchase their way into heaven by their donations to the church. Luther protested this practice of indulgences, but he was by no means the first or the only one to protest corruptions of the Roman church. Other reformers, such as John Wycliff and John Hus, were with him. But Luther it was who led the movement of revolt. Excommunicated and driven into hiding, he gave strong impetus to a protesting movement of Christians that later became the Protestant church.

The main theological premise of Luther's protest was that authentic Christian faith is not a matter of the mind's assent to a series of doctrines but the trust of the heart that, in God's gift of Christ, human sins are forgiven. For those who accept this atoning work of God's love, a new life is empowered, a life freed from the anxiety of attempting to lift oneself by one's own bootstraps to moral perfection into a new life of grace and freedom. That does not mean that the traditional moral rules of bodily self-discipline, charity, justice, honesty, fidelity in marriage, for instance, are cancelled. No. Rather, it means that they are practiced out of gratitude for God's grace. As he wrote, "Good works do not make a good man, but a good man does good works."

Luther's treatise "On Christian Liberty" spells out the manner in which the Christian is at once freed from the burden of the law and from the anxiety of self-reliance to be a "perfectly free Lord of all, subject to none" and also, by virtue of a reliance on God's grace, "a perfectly dutiful servant of all, subject to all." The authentic response to God's grace means a life of service that has "a regard to nothing except the needs and the advantage of the neighbor." Thus from God's gift of grace springs gracious living.

Another aspect of Luther's reform that profoundly influenced Protestantism was his doctrine of *Beruf*, or "calling." Catholic medieval culture had developed a two-tiered, split-level image of the Christian house of faith: on the upper level lived the religious —the monks, nuns, or priests—who had renounced the world and lived by the "counsels of perfection." On the first floor lived the "seculars," the laity—farmers, carpenters, tradesmen, housewives, even soldiers—who met the mundane needs and demands of the world. They were not secular in the sense that they were non-Christian, for they were to obey moral mandates of civil justice, but they were not committed to, nor could they live by, the perfect commands of the Gospel, the ascetic lives of chastity and poverty. Luther's doctrine of vocation smashed this two-storied scheme, at least in principle. All Christians, he said, in whatever walks of life, are called to serve neighbors in "the priesthood of all believers." All who experience grace are to be "Christs to their neighbors." Parent, merchant, farmer, pastor—all have equal status in the common-wealth of service.

The Reformed movement, sparked by Luther and others of like persuasion, spread through the Christian West. Europe became sharply divided into two hostile camps, Roman Catholic and Protestant. Within Protestantism there were many sectarian schisms. Holy wars were waged over which was the true faith, and the persecution and slaughter of heretics were common. One center of Protestant strength was Geneva, where John Calvin developed the seminal ideas of Luther and other reformers into a systematic theology entitled *Institutes of the Christian Religion*. His chief faith-premises were the absolute sovereignty of God and the pervasive original sin of humankind, from which one could be saved only by the grace of God's work in Christ. When turned from sin to a new life of trust, the true Christian is sustained by grace through the difficult ethical quandaries of choice. Calvin, who in his youth had law school training, gave greater place in the discipline of the Christian life to obedience to rules than Luther did.

The Locus of Authority

Another motif from Protestant history, highly important for its moral thought, concerns the locus of authority for ethics. Whereas in the Roman church, the "supreme court" of final authority centers in the Pope and the Councils of the church in Rome, in Protestant thought the locus shifts to the Bible. Over the centuries since Luther's revolt, just how the authority of Holy Scriptures is to be interpreted has been a matter of continued debate. Some take a fundamentalist view, as found in the majority of those in the Southern Baptist Convention and other conservative Protestants who are now termed of the "Religious Right," for whom the whole Bible is inerrant, from Genesis to Revelation. Others, in a more liberal spirit and aided by critical study of how Scripture came to be written, follow an intrabiblical norm, such as "the mind of Christ," or trust the guidance of the Spirit that interprets Scripture aright. Thus, some biblical truths are to be taken as more authoritative than others. The spirit, not the letter, of biblical laws becomes normative.

Change of Heart Versus Social Change

Other tension and debate continue in the development of Protestant ethics. Some stress the inner, private change of heart into a glad and trusting obedience as the essence of the Christian life, regardless of the outer circumstances in which the Christian lives. Martin Luther's doctrine of the two kingdoms, distinguishing the inner realm of grace and love and the outer realm of law and politics, gave some impetus to this way of thinking. Others stress that truly faithful obedience requires action to change the social

order. This accords with the biblical prophets who sought to help
the oppressed and release the captive. Changing radically the
capitalistic system of oppression and exploitation, seeking justice
in systems of penology, reducing the risk of nuclear war, and
supporting revolutions that seek genuine equality of rights for
minorities and women—these are the imperatives for Christian
living. The liberation theology movement of the latter part of this
century is a vivid example of this version of Protestant ethics, a
view shared by many Roman Catholics.

At first glance this rift seems so wide and deep as to make
reconciliation of the Protestant community impossible. A closer
look at the Protestant heritage, however, might lead us to recognize that there need not be a standoff between the pietists and the
social revolutionaries. The Christian life in its fullest sense involves
both the inner spirituality of a heart renewed by the grace of God,
which practices the disciplines of prayer and devotion, and the
movement from the altar to the marketplace and the polling booth,
which verifies its inner trust and faith and lives out its belief in
praxis, in daring witness to what God wills for the social order. The
integrity of Christian ethics in this Protestant form lies here: an
inner faith of a trusting heart active in outer witness and public
action.

The Issue of "Christ and Culture"

Still another way of explaining the differing versions of the
norms of the Christian life is based on the premise that tension
always exists between the radical moral demands of God in Christ
and the demands of the secular culture in which the Christian
lives. Differing Christian lifestyles are then explained by the way
Christians attempt to cope with this tension.[4] As formulated by the
German theologian Ernst Troeltsch in *The Social Teachings of the
Christian Churches*, a three-way difference has appeared in Christian history between, (1) the church-type understanding of the
relationship between the church and the world, in which accom-
modation to and compromise with worldly demands were
accepted and blessed as Christian, (2) the sect-type, in which with-
drawal and the rejection of worldly compromises in pure obe-

dience to God's commands become the marks of Christian living and in which communities are committed to this nonworldly lifestyle (e.g., the Amish or the Quakers), and (3) Christian mysticism, similar to the sect-type but more individualistic. Richard Niebuhr's *Christ and Culture* built on Troeltsch's typology, delineating not three but five differing ways in which Christians have tried to live within the tension between their mundane culture and the moral demands of God in Christ. At one extreme, "Christ against culture" is the ideal that renounces the world, the flesh, and the devil and tries to preserve its ethical virginity. The other extreme, "the Christ of culture," accommodates Christ to the various moral norms of secular culture, making him in effect the hero of secular values and thus resolving the tension. Between these two extremes, Niebuhr delineated three more types: "Christ above culture," best illustrated by the two-tiered scheme of medieval Catholicism, which has already been described; "Christ and culture in paradox," best represented by Luther's ethics, and finally "Christ transforming culture." Examples of this last type are the spirit of the Calvinistic and Puritan churches that sought to mold the political order after the model of God's kingdom of righteousness and the Protestant Social Gospel movement, which fought to transform the capitalistic economy from a competitive to a cooperative system of benevolent justice.

When one asks the question, "What does it mean to be a Christian?" one seems to hear at first a confusion of tongues, a babel of conflicting answers. Yet within that confusion remains an integrity of Christian ethics. Within the diversity is a shared faith-premise, a trust in God as the sovereign power over all, whose will for humankind is uniquely made known in Jesus Christ. Christian ethics consists in faithful and obedient response to that will by actions that seek the well-being of neighbors near and far. As in the great commandment, the love of God and the love of neighbor are joined. This is the "one" shared by the "many" versions, historical and contemporary, of the answers to the question, "What is Christian ethics?" It is this shared common faith that has brought the Protestant and Roman Catholic communities of faith much closer together than they were in the sixteenth and seventeenth centuries. The resolutions of Vatican II and of recent conferences of the World Council of Churches, representing mainline Protestantism, on the crucial issues of war, politics, economics, and ecology are strikingly similar. As James Gustafson has observed, the current "prospects for ecumenical Christian ethics are more encouraging than at any time since the Reformation."[5]

Protestant Ethics Today

The approach to Christian ethics in this introductory text is to delineate the distinctive Protestant reading of what constitutes the Christian life. There are points of accord and points of difference between the Protestant heritage and that of Roman Catholicism and also points of accord and difference between Protestant ethics and secular philosophical ethics.

There is not room here to trace the long story of Protestantism from the Reformation to the present, a story with many twists and turns.[6] The early Reformation of Luther and Zwingli was followed by Calvinism in Europe and Puritanism in England and America, represented by figures such as Richard Baxter and Jonathan Edwards. Then came the Evangelical movements, inspired by John Wesley and others, followed by the Christian Socialist school of thought in England and the Social Gospel movement in America, both addressing the economic problems of the industrial revolution of the late nineteenth and early twentieth centuries. Also in our century, the rise of neoorthodox theology and ethics, whose most influential voices were those of Karl Barth and Emil Brunner, called for a return to the radical Christocentric principles of the early Reformation. Currently, we are seeing a very popular movement of the neoevangelicals, or what is commonly called the new Religious Right, which champions the American values of free enterprise, capitalism, and the traditional patriarchal family unit against godless communism. At the other extreme are the liberation theologians, who call for freedom for those oppressed by reason of race, gender, or those lowest in the economic capitalistic power structure.

This diversity does not sound like a common voice. Yet within these wide divergencies in the understanding of Christian life, there remains a certain integrity, a genetic inheritance that churches of the Protestant tradition share in their liturgy, in their theological premises, and even in their social pronouncements. That integrity might be summarized briefly as follows:

(1) From Luther came the doctrine of justification by grace through faith. This still remains the point of divergence between Protestant and Roman Catholic moral theology, in which the achievement of salvation by good works remains a dominant theme, although the dialogue between Catholic and Protestant theologians is seeking to close this distance.

(2) God's saving grace has profound ethical consequence, for as one is continually turned from sin by God's forgiving grace—a process of *sanctification*, a term strong in Calvinism—one assumes responsibility for the well-being of neighbor and the disciplines of Christian virtue. Put in biblical terms, "We love because he first loved us."

(3) A third distinctive quality of the Protestant ethical heritage has to do with the locus of final authority. Whereas Roman Catholicism centers its authority in the hierarchy of Rome, the Pope, and the Councils of the Roman church in its reading of the objective order of natural law, Protestantism takes the Bible as its supreme court. Again, there are many differences as to just how the Bible is to be taken as authoritative. Fundamentalists take the whole Bible as universally true, inerrant; those of more liberal persuasion accept an inner-scriptural norm as authoritative, such as the "mind of Christ" or the Spirit, which interprets the Scriptures aright. Some types of Protestants extend the number of seats on the supreme court bench, as do United Methodists, with their quadrilateral authorities: "Scripture, tradition, reason, and experience."

(4) Finally, the political structures of the churches in the Protestant tradition are somewhat more democratic than the hierarchical structures of the Roman Catholic church. In Catholicism the magisterial authority of the Vatican in interpreting what is right and wrong, on matters of sexual ethics and divorce, for instance, leaves little room for conscientious dissent and debate. Protestantism, on the other hand, presumably has more room for

local congregational authority and, consequently, for divergence
on policy positions. In the dialectic of freedom and order, if
Catholicism leans toward strict order, Protestantism leans toward
freedom. Yet the policy statements on ethical issues from the
conferences of the World Council of Churches testify to a remark-
able degree of consensus among the mainline churches represented there.[7] The commonly shared understanding about the role
of the church in the world is that it should not be an escape from
the world but the social conscience of the world.

Protestant Ethics and Secular Moral Philosophy

Many points of affinity between Christian ethics and moral
philosophy rest on humanistic rather than theistic grounds. Much
of Aristotle's ethics, in its pursuit of *eudaimonia* ("well-being") is
evident in the scholastic ethics of St. Thomas Aquinas. The ethics
of Immanuel Kant, who based his norm of the categorical imperative on the authority of reason rather than revelation, nonetheless
is closely akin to the norm of the universal love of neighbor, which
is a central principle of Christian ethics. The sacred and equal right
and worth of all persons, basic to *The Humanist Manifesto*, is again
akin to the norms of biblical ethics as voiced by the prophets. One
influential contemporary humanistic ethical theory is that of John
Rawls, whose principles of fairness in *A Theory of Justice* closely
parallel the Christian theory of justice.

Christian ethics, both Protestant and Catholic, diverge from
secular, humanistic ethics, however, on the question of the foundation of human values.[8] The faith-premise of Christian ethics, as
shown in the following chapter, is a theonomous one. It rests on
the faith in revelation, the transcendent will of God. The faith-
premise of humanistic ethics is autonomous: the final authority of
human reason. In secular ethics, there is no transcendent norm of
responsibility and accountability, no divine will above human
history who sets the terms of the moral life.

Another interesting point of comparison is between utilitarian
ethics, as represented by Jeremy Bentham or John Stuart Mill, and
Christian ethics. The ultimate norm for Bentham was a hedonistic
one: according to him, human happiness could even be measured

quantitatively by a "hedonistic calculus." Mill had a qualitative theory of happiness: "It's better to be Socrates dissatisfied than a pig satisfied." At first glance the utilitarian norm of happiness seems to resemble the "blessedness" of which the Beatitudes speak in the Gospel. But on a closer look, the difference between utilitarian and Christian ethics becomes evident: in the Christian life the ultimate goal is not to seek happiness, singular or plural; rather, it is to be faithful to the will of God, even if that means suffering and pain. The blessedness to which the New Testament refers is not the goal, or aim, of living but the unsought by-product of faithful obedience to God's will.

3

The
Faith-Premises
of Christian Ethics

In chapter 1, I outlined briefly the way in which the secular "religions" of our culture have an implicit or explicit system of premises about how we know (epistemology), the nature of ultimate reality (ontology), the essence of human nature (anthropology), the character of the human predicament and its solution (soteriology), and the direction and destiny of human history (eschatology). All the ethical norms of the good life in these religions rest upon the syndrome of the faith-premises, which provide the answer to *why*, in the last analysis, this or that lifestyle is validated.

As we turn to the faith-premises of Christian ethics, we find a comparable relationship of ethics to certain faith-premises. The moral norms of Christian ethics depend upon foundational Christian theological assumptions. It is impossible to separate Christian ethics from Christian theology.[1]

My concern in this introductory text is to spell out the dependence of ethics on theology as distinctively understood in the Protestant tradition. There are, to be sure, many parallels with Roman Catholic ethics, as there are roots of Protestant morality in Judaism. Protestants should claim no monopoly on religious truths or ethical wisdom. But the distinctive slant developed in the succeeding pages is from the Reformed Protestant tradition.

Epistemology

We start with the problems of how reason and faith relate in the way we come to religious truth. The epistemology of scientism, as noted earlier, comes to its affirmations of truth by the inductive method, which is based on empirical evidence. When a Christian affirms, in the words of the familiar Creed, "I believe in God the Father Almighty, Maker of heaven and earth," this affirmation of faith has two sides. On one side it is a faith that God *is*: the assent of the *mind* to the reality of God's existence. On the other side is a trust of the *heart* in this One as the ultimate source of all. It is this aspect of faith that is most crucial in the Protestant tradition. All the way from Martin Luther through Søren Kierkegaard to Karl Barth, what counts is not so much the validity of theological arguments for the existence of God as it is a trust, a reliance on this transcendent One to sustain and renew one's life. It is belief *in* more than belief *that*. This existentialist aspect of faith assumes that human beings are by nature faithful beings, that is, persons whose hearts are where their treasures lie. Life is a long pilgrimage in search of the true source of security. The center of the heart's reliance may move from a teddy bear or a warm blanket to a college romance, to a career, to mammon, to the nation—or whatever. But for the long haul, this pilgrimage proves to be most often a path of disillusionment, one on which we discover that these gods are too finite and feeble to sustain us through dark days as well as bright days. Out of disillusionment with these finite centers of value, we may come to authentic faith and make the "leap of faith," as Kierkegaard calls it, to a trust in the Infinite One, beyond all the limited gods, as the One on whom we depend. This Infinite One has been the object of our heart's search all the way through the thickets and pitfalls of life's journey. As St. Augustine's prayer puts it, "Thou has created us for Thyself and our spirits are restless until they rest in Thee."

To some the epistemology of scientism is sharply opposed to that of the Christian faith. The current controversy between the proponents of scientific creationism and the proponents of evolution in public education, for example, seems to set critical reason against blind faith. On closer look, however, the two approaches to knowledge can be seen as parallel, not at odds. Underneath the whole scientific enterprise is a trust that there is an order within the whole array or disarray of data, an order that research seeks to discover. This trust is comparable to the Christian faith that there is unity, order, form, and meaning in the cosmos, an order not of human but of divine making.

Christian Ontology

Affirmations about the nature of God have been cast in many forms, some abstract and philosophical, such as "the Ground of Being" or "the First Cause." My approach in this book, however, is to use biblical imagery and metaphors, recognizing that they are mythical ways of speaking of God—myths, not in the sense of being false or fake, but in the sense of being told in poetic, graphic imagery derived from human experience that describes trans-human reality in idioms that cannot be caught by literal, empirical language. The use of biblical myths in speaking of God becomes dangerous when taken literally. But it is a rich way of capturing truths that underlie the empirical language of science.

The first ringing affirmation of the Creed is belief in the "Maker of heaven and earth." This doctrine of God as creator is simply an affirmation that all things, from snails to stars, are brought into existence by a power other than themselves. Creation is a continuing process that can be cast in the present tense as well as in the past. Moreover, the order of creation is not whimsical or arbitrary. It is reliable, faithful, trustworthy: "While the earth remains, seedtime and harvest, cold and heat, summer and winter, day and night, shall not cease" (Gen. 8:22). All human enterprise counts on this reliability of the created order. It signals the integrity of God. As Albert Einstein, a profoundly religious scientist, put it, "The Lord God may be subtle, but He is never mischievous."

Another aspect of the order of creation, as expressed in the mythology of Genesis 1, is that whatever is, is good in its original created nature. The order of being is the order of value. Also, in the grand scale of the order of creation, where, in biblical terms, human beings have a place "but little lower than the angels" and above "the birds of the air and the lilies of the field," our action is good when it befits our distinctively human place in the grand design of things. We infer such a scale of being when we exclaim in disgust about certain kinds of human behavior: "That's a beastly thing to do. It's degrading." Not that animals are bad in what they do, but that human beings should act in a way suitable to our higher place in the grand design of creation.

Christian Anthropology

Many aspects of the Christian view of human nature (or anthropology) can be inferred from what has just been said about the order of creation. In the grand design of all things, what is it that makes a person human? Philosophers and theologians have debated this question endlessly. Some would say that the distinctively human quality is *mind*. Persons are thinking animals who have the capacity for self-transcendence, memory, and foresight. (*Cogito, ergo sum*: "I think, therefore I am," as Descartes put it.) Others would say that the self is essentially *body*. The mind is only a complex network of interacting nerve cells in the brain. "I jog, therefore I am" would be a crude way of phrasing this physiological view of human nature.

Christian anthropology goes deeper. It accepts the view that we are bodies, frail and finite, made "out of the dust of the earth," and that we have minds, but it would not settle for either of these as the essence of our humanity. Underneath body and mind is a deeper reality that constitutes the core of selfhood: the heart, or will. This is Christian *voluntarism*, which does not mean freedom of choice but points to the *voluntas*, the heart, the will, as the core of self. This heart is not a physical organ, the blood-pumping machine in the chest that through the skill of medical science can now be transplanted from one human body to another. No, it means the will, or the total orientation of the self toward the object of affection. The core of who we are is to be defined by what we love. *Homo amans*: man loving. This *voluntas* is underneath body and mind. We act in a bodily sense as we will, and we think as we will. The link between this faith-premise and ethics becomes plain. The quality of moral action is determined by the direction of the will's object of affection. To quote St. Augustine again, "When there is a question as to whether a man is good, one does not ask what he believes, or what he hopes, but what he loves."

Still another feature of Christian anthropology is its view that persons are in their created nature persons-in-community, social selves. As the mythology of Genesis puts it, God created Eve to be a helpmate for Adam. This corporate view is neither the kind of radical individualism, the "loner" view that may be found in some versions of Protestant thought, nor the kind of collectivism that makes a person simply one case in a collective mass, as in Marxist communism. Normatively speaking, the Christian view of persons-in-community is always corporate, for "no [one] is an island entire of itself," as John Donne expressed it. Christian ethics is thus always in some sense social ethics. "Horizontal" relationships with other persons are as inevitable an aspect of Christian life as the "vertical" relationships of a person with the Creator God.

Covenant Theology and Human Sin

Another key concept in the biblical faith about the order of creation is that of covenant.[2] God as creator sets the terms of community. As Deuteronomy 30:15–17 phrases it, "See, I have set before you this day life and good, death and evil. If you obey the commandments of the LORD your God . . . then you shall live . . . and the LORD your God will bless you. . . . But if you . . . are drawn away to worship other gods . . . you shall perish." Obedience to the terms of the covenant leads to the blessing of true community; disobedience leads to the curse of broken community.

The terms of the covenant are severe and stern. God as creator endows human beings with the gift of a "dreadful" freedom of choice to obey or disobey the Commandments. But it is a freedom among forced options, because we are not free *not* to choose and not free from the consequences of choice. Here we encounter another feature of the manner of God's rule and of the human response to it, one that is especially underscored in Protestant ethics: human sin. The word *sin* is in our secular culture casually dismissed as a hangover from our Puritan past,[3] or in common parlance it is confused with bodily self-indulgences: "wine, women, and song." But the core meaning of *sin* is "hubris," "pride," in which the will rebels against God's sovereignty and the terms of his covenant and is turned inward in radical egocentricity.[4] This appears not only in private relationships, for example, in a man's sexual abuse of a woman, but also in public relationships: the sins of ethnocentrism, racial pride, class pride, national pride, or ecclesiastical pride, by which we put down those of another color, class, nationality, or church affiliation. Hubris is the sinister, all-pervasive infection of will that disrupts the community of the created order and sets persons or groups against each other.

But persons who live in rebellion against God's rule and defy the terms of covenant are still citizens of his kingdom, and their betrayal thus brings them under the judgment of God. Again, the dark aspect of God's rule—God as governor and judge—should not be read to mean that God punishes human sin by zapping adulterers with lightning bolts or by inflicting cancer on a child as punishment for some sin that a parent has committed. No, not "interventionist" judgment. Rather, God governs, overrules, and punishes human prides of all sorts through the inexorable consequences that follow from human sin, consequences that a social scientist or an agronomist or a psychologist can trace. If we despoil our natural environment by exploiting the soil, the garden becomes a wasteland, and the feedback to sustain life is endangered or destroyed. If a marriage is simply a contest of colliding egos, tension and misery for the children are inevitable. If a dominant power or class in the state denies equal rights to a minority group, community is broken, and the deprived group will lash out in riots and rebellion. All these are illustrations of God's "consequential"

judgment. Though the process may be tardy and "the sins of the
fathers . . . visited upon the children," still, sooner or later, "the
wages of sin is death."

Christian Soteriology

God's judgment is not the last word, however. Christian
theology has a further aspect: the doctrine of salvation. The One
God who creates the order of all things in harmony, who sets the
terms of covenant, who governs and overrules the sin of humanity
in disobedience to the covenant, is also a God of grace, who
restores life to harmony and peace: God as redeemer. What is the
relationship of God's action as judge to God's action as redeemer?
The integrity of Christian monotheism precludes a schizoid theology, in which God's left hand of wrath does not know what his
right hand of mercy is doing. No, seen through the trusting eyes of
the Christian faith, the punishments and chastisements in human
history are corrective. God is a demanding but loving father. He
punishes in order to restore. This does not mean "cheap grace" that
overlooks all human corruptions and says, "Forget it." Grace does
not mean the indulgence of sin. God's hand in mercy does more,
not less, than what God's hand in judgment exacts. Grace exists,
even within the chastisements of history, as a loving father seeks
to correct and redeem a child through strict discipline.

The concept of God's redeeming grace in the Protestant tradition, especially in Calvinism, has been understood at two levels:
"common grace" and "special grace." Common grace refers to a
trust in a divine impulse in all nature and in all human affairs to
restore order and harmony out of disorder. In the natural environment, for instance, nature has the recuperative power to restore
soil, forests, streams of water, to ecological health, after human
exploitation has abused and polluted them. In human affairs, there
is a drive for the recovery of concord out of discord, peace out of
war, reconciliation of opposing factions and nations. These are
signals of a divine redeeming grace.

The special grace of the Christian faith is seen in the figure of
Jesus Christ. The space here, however, is inadequate for an exami-
nation of the many different Christologies, as they are called, in the
history of Christian thought.

The classical, legal Anselmic doctrine affirms that because human sin is against the Infinite God, it can only be atoned for by the death of God-in-Christ on the cross, thereby making retribution. The classical Protestant Reformers, such as Luther and Calvin, described salvation as the process in which the heart of the believer is turned from self-reliance to God-reliance by the work of Christ, or "justification by faith." Evangelical Protestants such as John Wesley affirmed that the forgiving grace of God clears the heart from sin and sets the Christian on the path of perfection, a new life in Christ, which issues in the love of neighbor and which "never flowed from any fountain but gratitude to our Creator." The more modern types of Christology center on the human Jesus of the Gospels, "the young and fearless prophet," who dared to challenge the religious establishment of his day in the name of social justice for the oppressed and who provides inspiration for those in our own day who would be his disciples by following his example. A common theme shared by traditional and modern Christologies is the affirmation, to use St. Paul's words, "God was in Christ reconciling the world to himself" (2 Cor. 5:19). Or as the writer to the Ephesians said, "he has broken down the dividing wall of hostility . . . so making peace" (Eph. 2:14).

Salvation in the Protestant heritage is not something earned or merited by works but is a gift that turns the self outward from its egocentricity, from its anxious self-dependence into God-dependence, into a new life—one of gracious living, in response to the grace of God, a life of true freedom, which means freedom for a life of moral responsibility.

Note, by the way, that God's actions as creator, judge, and redeemer are not to be understood *seriatim,* one after the other in time, but as simultaneous. God does not create on Monday, judge on Tuesday, redeem on Wednesday. At any one moment or epochal event in history, the eyes of faith can discern in what is happening in nature and human affairs the creative activity of God, the abuse of creation and covenant by human sin, with the consequent penalties of God's judgment, but also the gracious hand of mercy and forgiveness. Such was Abraham Lincoln's reading of the events near the end of the Civil War, as expressed in his second inaugural address.

Christian Eschatology

Finally, what of the Christian faith-premise concerning the direction and end (or *eschaton*) of human history? Here, also, many different answers to the question are forthcoming. Devout Protestants who believe in the literal inerrancy of the Bible can expect soon a cataclysmic *eschaton*, the close of the age, by some miraculous intervention of God, as the book of Revelation foretells.

A secular version of this dark eschatology, by the way, is voiced by the prophets of doom among the scientific community, who warn that we are perilously close to the end of history, an end that will come, not by divine intervention, but by human blunders in the use of high technology, which will destroy all life on earth in a nuclear holocaust, making the earth uninhabitable in a nuclear winter.

A very different answer is the eschatological hope of liberal Protestantism, such as was voiced by proponents of the Social Gospel, who read history as the gradual movement of humankind toward the perfect kingdom of God realized on earth, the kingdom of peace and righteousness and justice, when "earth shall be fair and all her folk be one." It is this hope for a blessed future that bends the bow of moral campaigns for radical social change. The buoyant hope that such a utopia is a realistic eschatology, however, has been clouded, if not shattered, by the tragic events of the twentieth century.

What faith-premise about the direction and end of human history remains plausible then? Prophecies about the future, dark or bright, are futile. What does seem certain is that human history is a constant, churning admixture of good and evil, of human weal and woe. Advances in medical and agricultural sciences improve the human lot, but they bring in their wake new difficulties. As Reinhold Niebuhr often reminded us, "A new evil rides in on the back of every good." Then the new evil becomes a challenge to be met with a new good, which in turn becomes corrupted by its own excesses. Any period of human history is roughly equidistant from both utopia and dystopia, as any moment in time is equidistant from eternity.

The implication of this eschatological position for Christian ethics is that the basic motivation for ethical action is shifted from hope to faith. The mainspring of human choices in the maelstrom of goods and evils is how to respond fittingly to God's action as creator, judge, and redeemer in this time, whatever the outcome. The question to be asked of the Christian in the final analysis (or, to use biblical mythology, at the judgment seat) is not "Were you successful?" but "Were you faithful?" We are back to the Reformed doctrine: the just shall live by faith. The moral quality of human life is to be measured by the degree to which we act in faithful and trusting response to God's sovereignty, seeking first his kingdom and his righteousness. The crucial question for ethics then is not the speculative one: how will it all wind up at the end? No, the question is, how shall we discern and do God's will on the earth now?

4

Christian
Ethical Norms

Any competent architect, having seen the blueprints for the foundation of a building, can make a fairly exact prediction of what the superstructure would be like. Here also, from the layout of the theological foundations already discussed, one can anticipate the likely shape of Christian ethical norms in the superstructure of the house of faith. The syndrome of moral "oughts," based on these foundations, can be best seen as responses to the ways in which God's creative, governing, and redeeming power is interpreted and acted upon.

Response to God as Creator

The first ethical response to God's continual creation of a universe of beauty and order is praise and gratitude. A doxology of mind and heart, voiced or silent, is from first to last along the vertical plane the response from which spring all the other ethical norms of Christian living along the horizontal plane. From sunrise

to sunset and "through the watches of the night," as the psalmist says, "The Lord's name is to be praised." To put it in Calvinistic phrasing, "the chief end of man is to glorify God and enjoy him forever."
But the order of creation as gift and endowment is given as a sacred trust to human beings who have the power of decision as to how the order of creation should be used. True worship, then, does not consist only in a doxology. It also involves the responsible stewardship of creation, the care and nurture of the created order. Indeed worship is not authentic if it is only a solemn bow before the altar, in reverent praise or in the reception of the sacraments. For as such Old Testament prophets as Amos cried out, attacking the religious ceremonies of his day, God takes no delight in

"solemn assemblies. . . .
Take away from me the noise of your songs;
to the melody of your harps I will not listen.
But let justice roll down like waters,
and righteousness like an ever-flowing stream" (Amos 5:23–24).

In the same prophetic tradition, Jesus challenged the strict sabbatarian laws of his day by performing acts of healing and mercy on the sabbath. For Christ, the true way to keep the sabbath holy was to care for those in need.
The ethics of stewardship, as response to continual creation, may be understood at three levels: care of the natural environment, care of neighbor, and care of self. All these are implied in the great commandment of the Jewish Torah, which Jesus reminded his critics was the basis of all of the particular laws. "You shall love the Lord your God with all your heart, and with all your soul, and with all your strength, and with all your mind; and your neighbor as yourself" (Luke 10:27).
Care for the natural environment, the garden of Eden, which Adam was charged "to till and to keep," is the basis of a Christian ecological ethic. The ethical problems of ecology in our industrial culture are addressed in some detail in a later chapter. Here, let me say only that the normative view of how we should treat our natural environment is not the worship of nature as such, but the

responsible use of nature for human well-being in accountability
to the Creator, both for present generations and those yet to come.

The Christian Meaning of Love

Christian love links ecological ethics to the second part of the
great commandment: love of neighbor. Here we walk into a jungle
of semantic confusion about the meaning of the word *love*. Our
secular, commercial culture has desecrated the word so that it
means a host of things—sexual attraction, fellow-feeling, patriotism, the *gemütlichkeit* induced by Pabst Blue Ribbon beer—that
have little if anything to do with Christian love. Analyzing the
semantic meanings of the word *love* as it appears on the Valentine
cards at the drugstore or on a day's run of TV commercials would
be a confusing and depressing exercise indeed.

Christian love, or agape, is something radically different from
its common uses in commercial spoilage.[1] It has to do first of all
with the inner heart or intention, not with outer, visible action. The
distinctive quality of agape is derived from the "center of value" by
which a person is treated, or the "middle term" between self and
another. In Christian love, that center of value is nothing finite or
limited, not a closed circle, not love for those in our circle, in Pi Beta
Phi, in our alma mater, in the First Presbyterian Church, or love for
our race, our class, our nation. No, Christian agape is of a heart that
loves the other in God. God is the middle term between self and
others. It is regard for the other person simply as a precious
creation of God, on the common ground of creatureliness. In
Christian love I am responsible to God for neighbors, near and far,
all members of the human family. In short, agape is theocentric
neighbor-love.

This God-centered definition has several implications. For
one, Christian love means a care for the particular person in his or
her distinct individuality, since that person confronts me in the
order of creation as one who is unlike any other person. My regard
for a person, or for a group of persons, ought never to be for cases
of color, of class, of nationality, of belonging in such and such a tax
bracket. Christian love is personal, sensitive to all the shades of
difference that make us in creation as unlike as we are like.

A second implication of this concept of God-centered neighbor-love is that it is disinterested. Not uninterested, but disinterested in the sense that it engages in all the commerce of social transactions but not with the primary motive, "What's in this deal for me, or for my group?" Paul's classic definition of *agape* in First Corinthians says, "Love seeketh not its own." Here *agape* is distinct from *eros*. For eros, taking it in the higher sense than libidinal, sexual desire, is love that is ultimately turned in on itself, seeking its own happiness, or self-realization, or heavenly reward, the love of the operator, who in all the deals of kindness and apparent service is playing the anxious and shrewd game of one-upmanship.

A third implication of this ideal of God-centered neighbor-love is that it is indiscriminate and inclusive in the scope of its care. Agape is personal, sensitive to the distinct uniqueness of individuals, yes, but it is not "fastidious," as Kierkegaard put it, or selective in the lines it draws as to who is in or who is outside the circle of concern. Agape differs from *philia*, the Greek term for friendship, which means "the attraction of like for like," as "birds of a feather flock together," an affection based on affinities. This affection is not morally wrong. It is one of the positive joys of human relations and certainly one of the bonds of a secure marriage. But it is not agape. Many sharp statements in the New Testament confirm the distinction between *philia* and agape. In one of his parables, Jesus identified the one who proved neighbor to the man who fell among the thieves as the good Samaritan. In that day, a Samaritan was the hated outlander, the unlike, despised by Jews. Yet it was he, not the priest or the Levite, who showed agape. Luke 14:12–14 makes the same point: "When you give a dinner or a banquet, do not invite your friends or your brothers or your kinsmen or rich neighbors, lest they also invite you in return. . . . But when you give a feast, invite the poor, the maimed, the lame, the blind, and you will be blessed, because they cannot repay you."

Indiscriminate concern for all, like and unlike, friend and enemy, is a faithful response to the love of God, who in creation is not fastidious but who "makes his sun rise on the evil and on the good, and sends rain on the just and the unjust" (Matt. 5:45).

A final implication of this understanding of agape as the supreme moral norm of Christian ethics is that although it is indiscriminate as to *whom* it loves, it is discriminating in *how* it loves. This crucial aspect of the norm of stewardship is often forgotten. God in creation entrusts others—my children, students in my class, my fellow citizens—to my responsible care, and I as steward am accountable to God for their well-being. I am obliged by love to seek their good as best I can. This requires judgments and decisions that may distinguish between what the other person *needs* and what he or she *wants*. Here agape differs from sentimental indulgence and complete permissiveness, which can be heard in the parental wail, "We don't know what's the matter with Emma Lou. We give her everything she wants." That's precisely what *is* the matter with Emma Lou. There is an element of stringency, of discipline, of rigor, in agape that makes it different from "luhve."

Love as Self-Regard

"Love your neighbor as yourself." Given the distinctive qualities of disinterestedness in agape, it would seem that as a moral norm it would rule out any regard for self. True, the radical egocentricity of the ego-beaver would revise the great commandment to read "Love your neighbor *for* yourself." When the "I" is, in effect, the ultimate object of concern, it acts against the norm of Christian love. But another form of self-regard is suggested in the last phrase of the great commandment. In the order of creation, my body, my brains, my talents, my possessions, my psyche, are given to me by God as a precious entrustment. I ought to be steward of myself and take care of myself so that I may be a fit instrument to serve the common good. Agape therefore includes theocentric self-regard. It is in keeping with the spirit of Christian love to adopt a lifestyle of good health habits, of growth of mind and spirit, to acquire mechanical or artistic skills, to obey, in short, the casual admonition we use in passing: "Take care."

We should recognize, however, that in some life situations the needs of neighbor and the regard for self collide, that one may have to cut back on one's own well-being to serve another's good, and that radical self-denial and self-sacrifice are called for. Here is the highest cruciform level of agape, the love of the one who gives up his or her life for another, in obedience to the radical commands of Jesus Christ. But those also are his faithful followers who take as their norm the stewardship of self—theocentric self-care.

From all that has been said about agape, it is plain that it is a high ideal, a moral norm rarely lived out. Few indeed are the saints who have embodied this norm in total single-hearted obedience to the great commandment. Church folk talk easily about the practice of Christian love and concern, but the motives in their hearts are a very mixed bundle. Yet agape remains the norm by which we judge and measure all our lesser loves, in the moral ambiguities that make up the complexities of our hearts' desires both in our private relations and in our public policies.

Response to God as Judge

The world I encounter in my daily round is, however, far from the given order of creation. We live far east of Eden, in what Protestant theology traditionally has called a fallen world. The morning paper brings news of gross cruelties, hijacking by terrorists, wars and rumors of wars, rampant poverty and hunger abroad and at home, alcoholism and drug addiction close by, as well as deceptions and graft in high economic and political offices. It is a world that seems, as it did to Martin Luther, "with devils filled, that threaten to undo us."

In the preceding chapter I tried to delineate how the Christian reads these tragic current events through the eyes of faith. They are the consequences of human abuse of the order of creation, the dire results of human sin, which bring in their inexorable wake the results of human misery: God's judgment. What then should be the ethical response to God's rule as judge?

The response has two facets. The first is contrition and repentance, the acknowledgment of the heart that we are sinners who daily violate the terms of covenant in ways we manage cleverly to hide from others and from ourselves. In a chapel or church service we delude ourselves into thinking we are righteous. Like the parable of the Pharisee and the Tax Collector in Luke 18:10–14, we may say with the Pharisee, "God, I thank thee that I am not like other men." We contrast our virtue with the vices of others. We may even join heartily in singing "Amazing grace . . . That saved a wretch like me." But no one honestly feels that he or she is really a wretch.

Against self-righteousness, the response of the Christian to divine judgment is the acknowledgment of one's own sin—all the ways that in pride, in greed, in racial, chauvinistic, political prejudice, we contribute to the disorder of human society. This vertical response of contrition becomes the spring of a lifestyle that tries to cope with the corruptions and disorders of the home, the economic or political order, and international relations, along the horizontal plane.

The restraint of sin, the coercive use of power in dealing with crime in the streets, with the violation of civil rights, or with vandalism and terrorism, is a necessary response of faithful Christian ethics to God's judgment. But not just any old coercion. There are two crucial ingredients in the Christian restraint of sin. One is that the restrainer holds himself or herself to the same standard of judgment that he or she exacts of another, for as Christ's words remind us, "With what measure you judge, you will be judged." We are under a universal judgment. Our God is not a respecter of persons. Therefore, self-correction must accompany the correction of others. For example, dealing with crime among juvenile delinquents in an inner-city ghetto, the police department of a city must enforce the law and exact penalties for the crimes committed. But at the same time the city officials should acknowledge their own complicity and blame. They have contributed to these crimes in their failure to provide decent housing, education, and employment. So it becomes not a matter of saints who are punishing sinners, but of sinners who are correcting sinners.

Response to Grace

The second facet of a Christian ethical response in dealing with both the private and the systemic expressions of sin is that it is a will to restore, to redeem, to rehabilitate. This moral norm is faintly echoed in the fact that the police departments of our cities are not called Departments of Punishment but Departments of Correction.

The ultimate intent in all forms of discipline, punishment, and restraint that parents may impose on their children or that the state may impose on criminals or that indeed nations may be forced to use in dealing with each other is reconciliation or the restoration of community. And this is response to the third form of the rule of God: his redeeming grace. For, as noted earlier, the final word we affirm about God's activity in history is the word of grace, forgiveness, and redemption.

Faithful ethical response to the grace of God involves the will to seek the restoration of community when it has been strained or broken off by human sin. In families, for instance, wise parents are gracious in their discipline of their children, as when they forgive their children's trespasses and recover the loving bond of community in the home. Out of a single-hearted love, Christian parenting can at once cherish, restrain, and forgive a child. The policies of criminal justice by which the decisions of the courts or prison officials impose monitored paroles or sentences that require community service are expressions of the ethics of grace. They attempt to turn prisons from schools of crime, which most of them now are, into schools of education that can restore the offender to responsible citizenship. One such program in a Minnesota state prison, called Insight, enables inmates to earn a college degree while serving their time in prison. The evidence shows that when such policies of rehabilitation are followed, the rate of recidivism, that is, repetition of criminal offenses and prison sentences, is markedly reduced.

Again, realism requires us to acknowledge that this gracious will to forgiveness and reconciliation may not always succeed. The enemy may not be turned from enmity to friendship, and the battle may not have a happy ending. But the moral worth of this ethic stands nonetheless, in success or failure, because we are judged not by the outcome but by the degree of our fidelity to the will of God.

As spelled out in some detail later, the ethics of forgiveness in response to God's grace in Christ becomes more and more difficult to practice as one moves from the inner circle of family life to the larger circles of national and international relations. But there is no boundary where the normative ethics of grace and forgiveness stops and another ethic of rigid retribution begins. Humankind is one family under one Father, One Lord of all, who is forever creating, governing, judging, and redeeming the whole order of life.

5

Christian Love and Social Justice

In chapter 2, I outlined the foundational premises of faith as they have been understood in the Christian tradition, with certain features especially stressed in the Protestant heritage. There are variants, to be sure, within this heritage—Lutheran, Calvinistic, evangelical, Social Gospel—but all share an identity in their affirmation that the good life consists in faithful and trusting obedience to the will of God, as that will is manifest in Jesus Christ.

The central virtue of the Christian life as defined in chapter 4 is agape, whose distinguishing qualities rest upon the theological faith-premises about God's sovereignty as creator, governor, and redeemer.

I should note in passing that in other systems of ethical theory the principle of love of neighbor as a key virtue rests on secular faith-premises, such as the sacred and inviolable worth of persons, which is a humanistic premise, or a utilitarian premise that the practice of such love is conducive to the general happiness. Christianity should claim no exclusive monopoly in understanding or practicing the virtue of love. This acknowledgment, however, in no wise invalidates the assertion that for the Christian community the ultimate validation and ground for love is a transcendent one, the divine will.

Now, turning from the altars of worship and the convictions of heart and mind to face the facts, we confront immediately a welter of problems in the empirical circumstances that surround us, so baffling as to make the simple, direct application of the norm of love difficult if not impossible to realize. But ethical choices, for better or worse, must be made.

For example, I am driving along an interstate highway and notice a forlorn hitchhiker, his thumb pointing at a familiar angle, wanting a ride in the direction I am headed. What should be my response of conscience? Perhaps Gospel injunctions come to mind: "Give to him who asks of you" or "Inasmuch as you did it to one of the least of these my brethren, you did it unto me." But a second look gives me pause. The hitchhiker looks tough and scruffy. Into my head flash gory news accounts of victims of hitchhikers who were assaulted and murdered and then locked in the trunk of the car. It's illegal for him to be hitchhiking on an interstate, anyway. Should I risk my own well-being for his sake, or should I take care of myself? Perhaps also my responsibility to the well-being of my own family comes into the moral nexus of choice. By the time my conscience has sorted out the pros and cons of whether or not I should show concern for this one needy neighbor, and prove a good Samaritan, I am three miles past him on the highway. No point now in turning around.

The Baffling Context of Choices

This illustrates in a one-on-one neighbor relationship the issues that multiply exponentially as one moves into plural neighbor relations. "Love your neighbor." Yes, but *which* neighbors? In the context of choice, many neighbors crowd in upon the conscience with competing needs. It is impossible to serve all of them. The cultural revolutions of recent centuries, especially the technological revolution, have radically changed the context of choice from what it was in biblical times, when *neighbors* meant those who lived nearby. Now, technology in communication and travel has brought the far neighbor near, as near as the turn of the TV dial, compounding enormously the problem of competing neighbor claims. The morning mail delivers nine appeals from organizations that recount graphic, woeful tales of starving children or battered women or Native Americans deprived of their land rights—all pleading for my support. To which of these neighbors should my money go? Another dimension of the problem is the collision between the protection of God's good earth against developers who invade the wilderness and turn the garden of Eden into a wasteland of a commercial strip. Yet this economic development provides employment for neighbors who need jobs. In setting international trade policies, should the protectionists set high tariffs to protect American textile or automobile workers against cheaper imports, or should a free trade policy, with no barriers, serve the livelihood of textile or auto workers abroad? Or in politics—local, state, and national—the choices that must be made are never morally clear and unambiguous, between a party or candidate who represents the pure Christian ideal and an opposing candidate or party who represents Satan. Political choices always lie in the grey area between pure good and dark evil. Yet political decisions have to be made. Not to choose becomes itself a form of choice. Obviously, it becomes romantic and irresponsible to go blithely into the arenas of daily life, domestic, economic, political, racial, international, equipped only with the simple prescription "Love your neighbor."

Double Contextualism

Therefore it becomes necessary to think out a more realistic, careful structure of Christian decision making that can translate the norm of love into practice.[1] One plausible structure or model for doing ethics between the faith and the facts, between the constraints of the descriptive "is" and the normative "ought," might be diagrammed as follows.

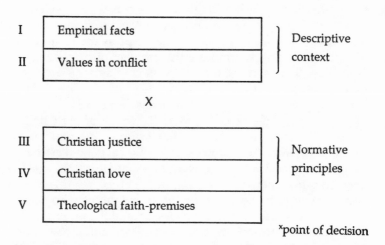

It becomes ridiculous, to be sure, to diagram Christian ethics in geometric terms, to analyze the confusing problems of hard choice in terms of a five-tiered cake. The schema is suggested, however, to show how responsible ethical decision (marked by the X) is made at the interface between the descriptive context, the situation of a person's decision on the one hand, and the normative ethical principles one is obliged to fulfill on the other. These norms are validated by the basic theological premises already discussed. To repeat, responsible choice is made at the interface between the faith and the facts.

Ideally, of course, Christian ethical decision would move from the bottom up, from the convictions of faith as to the terms of God's covenant (V), expressed in the intention to do God's will in agape (IV), translating that love into a sensitive justice (III) as it confronts the conflicting values (II) within the hard facts (I) of the situation of choice, which more often than not puts one between a rock and a hard place.

It may clarify this approach to Christian decision, however, to move from the top down and to show the interrelationship of levels I through V. Bear in mind, of course, that this sequence is not to be understood chronologically, like a time line, but psychologically, since plainly one stands between the faith and the facts at the same time and must take account of both in the crucible of choice.

It may clarify the issue of decision making to spell out, in some detail, what is involved in each of these levels.

Look first at the descriptive levels.

Level I: Empirical Facts

Responsible Christian decision should be as informed concerning the hard facts of the cultural context of choice as it is faithful to what God in Christ requires. When faced with hard choices in domestic affairs, in medical or business practices, in ecclesiastical policy, in political choices, we must in Christian action learn as much as possible about the limiting or permissive circumstances that surround the choice to be made.

A major contribution was made to the development of Christian ethics when, earlier in this century, ethicists such as Bishop John Robinson and Joseph Fletcher advanced a school of thought that came to be known as situation ethics.[2] Fletcher in particular protested the kind of inflexible Christian legalism that would apply some Christian law from the Bible or the church to a situation of choice that had radically changed from the time when the precept was mandated. However, in its preoccupation with the changing circumstances and its inclination to derive the moral "ought" almost solely from the empirical "is," situation ethics proved in time to slide down a slippery slope toward the ethics of improvisation and become normless.[3] But its realism in acknowledging an initial responsibility in Christian decision to know the facts, the lay of the land, is nonetheless an essential part of moral wisdom.

Level II: Values in Conflict

Level II, still in the descriptive context, is an attempt to assess the values in conflict in the factual circumstances. The plain facts of a domestic or urban or rural or business situation are not simply statistics, value-free. No, every situation of human interrelation is value-laden. All sorts of considerations of what is good or bad, right or wrong, beneficial or harmful, are embedded in the data. The values at stake in every situation can be understood in three dimensions.

What values? Philosophers and theologians inside and outside the Christian tradition have articulated in many different ways the hierarchy of values that constitute the good life. The consensus is that there are foundational values of life and health, which are provided by daily bread and a minimum of economic security. But to be fully human, persons "shall not live by bread alone." The middle-range values are the social values of friendship and concord. Then there are higher values: aesthetic, intellectual, and spiritual. The truly good life would be one in which the total range of these values would be realized. The trouble is, of course, by reason of human finitude, cultural limitations, and an inheritance of wrong choices, these values collide. Some must be short-changed in preference to others. What college student has not had to sacrifice sleep to complete a research paper by the deadline? Or one may have to abandon a high aesthetic or intellectual pursuit in order to secure money to live on. Economic values and spiritual values often collide.

The second level of the value collision is the time dimension in which current values conflict with future values. Life's daily decisions involve risk-benefit choices between the sure good of "a bird in the hand" versus the possible greater good of "two in the bush." How much should one risk present security in the prospect of realizing a higher security in the future? This value collision is present in much more than investment choices of stocks and bonds. We are often baffled about deciding between two maxims: "He who hesitates is lost" against "Wait till the time is ripe." It also appears as a tension in ecological decisions where current prosperity is pitted against the security of posterity, which we would sacrifice at our present level of consumption. How much should we mortgage the future to live well now?

The third dimension of the values in conflict is the most crucial in Christian ethical theory: whose values? Here again, human choices are squeezed between serving the needs of some neighbors versus the needs of other neighbors, when, in an economy of scarcity, it is impossible to serve them all. The conventional Christian moral platitude calls us to love all humankind. But the forced options are never between meeting and denying universal needs. The actual situation of choice is to provide for the good of some neighbors or to provide for the good of other neighbors. We have to rob Peter to pay Paul. The tightest decisions are those in which the needs and rights of some collide with the needs and rights of others. This dilemma confronts me daily in handling my finances. Should I pay a high tuition bill to secure the best possible education for my children, or should I heed the desperate appeals for money to feed hungry children in Africa when my income cannot afford both? It is present in the value collision in the abortion debate, between the rights of the unborn fetus and the rights of the mother, perhaps even her life. And it moves out to the international problems of foreign policy in Central America or in the Middle East. As the wry lines of Robert Frost expressed it:

> But even where, thus, opposing interests kill,
> They are to be thought of as opposing goods
> Oftener than as conflicting good and ill;
> Which makes the war god seem no special dunce
> For always fighting on both sides at once.[4]

All three dimensions of this value conflict—what, when, and whose—may be entailed in any one moral quandary that puzzles the conscience at the juncture of decision.

Level III: Christian Justice

Realistic Christian ethics, confronting the tight ethical dilemmas posed in the value collisions just described, cannot jump straight from Christian agape into the matrix of decision and simply do the loving thing. What is needed is the middle panel (III), Christian justice, to bridge the gap between Christian love and the limiting circumstances of choice. Christian justice translates the norm of agape into responsible guidelines for deciding in the squeeze of competing values.

The history of Christian ethical theory has encompassed many different persuasions about the relationship of love and justice as moral norms. One tradition of thought, deriving from Martin Luther's theory of the two kingdoms, separates the two sharply. The spirit of love is kindness, tenderness, forgiveness, sympathy, warmth, which are appropriate in personal relationships as the fruit of a life forgiven by God's grace in Christ. The spirit of justice, on the other hand, is equity, retribution, balance, discipline for wrongs done, which are appropriate in the impersonal dealings of government with its citizens or in the disciplinary practices of a school administration. Tender love is the norm for Christian living at home. Stern justice is the norm for Christian policy in public, in the marketplace, or in the courts of law. The two do not mix. Lutheran ethics tends to split the inner heart of a person's gracious love from what a person's outer office as magistrate or soldier requires. But such a dualism violates the integrity of the Christian life. It runs against the Hebraic norm of righteousness, which calls us "to do justly, to love mercy, and to walk humbly before God," in public as much as in private affairs. We may grant with the heirs of the Lutheran tradition that there is indeed a tension that should trouble a Christian judge, a tension between one's compassion toward the criminal offender and one's duty to uphold the law. But a totally split ethic is far off the normative mark.

Yet also far off the mark is the easy resolution of this tension proposed by Joseph Fletcher, who claimed that "love and justice are the same, for justice is love distributed, nothing else."[5] That is to say, for Fletcher, the same norm that informs our agape concern for the single neighbor is extended to many neighbors. It is simply multiplied from the singular to the plural. But this monism trips over the problem of competing neighbor claims and rights. It is impossible to do justice to all, near and far, even if we could do full justice to one person.

Between a radical dualism, splitting love from justice, and a simple monism, melting them into one, is a more realistic alternative that holds love and justice in dialectical tension. Christian justice is the proximate realization of love under the limiting circumstances of choice among competing values. The moral imperative of Christian justice is to seek the highest possible quality of life for the widest possible range of persons. Such a norm takes into account the three dimensions of the value collision mentioned above: what, when, and whose. The positive aspect of the dialectic is that such justice is "tempered with mercy." It has the pull of agape upon it. The negative aspect of the dialectic is that, given the moral economy of scarcity, a distance always remains between what pure love would do and what any particular social policy of justice can do under the limitation of circumstances.

A realistic and responsible Christian social ethic stresses the positive connection in this dialectic between love and justice. Three aspects of the norm of justice, whether defined in the distributive or retributive sense, derive from the spirit of love.

One is *impartiality*. Our practical wisdom is morally correct in calling "just" the decision of an umpire or of a judge in a court case or of the school board, if it is impartial, unbiased, and unprejudiced. When a judge disqualifies himself or herself in a certain case because of a conflict of interest, that decision is respected as a mark of impartiality and fairness. The Christian ground of such impartiality is precisely the disinterestedness of agape, a love that "seeketh not its own," as St. Paul defined it, detached from self-seeking, or from partiality toward one's own party, nation, class, race. Such a disinterested love in turn rests upon the theological faith-premise: God is the ultimate center of value and concern. Allegiance to his rule transcends every finite human partiality.

A second component in justice is *equality*. We resonate to such slogans as "equal rights for all," "equal pay for equal work," "equal justice under the law." All these express a norm that a just society is one in which all persons stand on a par. The justice that starts from this baseline of equality is the indirect expression of agape in the sense that all persons are equally creatures of God and should be treated as such. Here the indiscriminate quality of agape stands as the foundation of equality in justice. In contrast to "fastidious" love, to use Kierkegaard's term, which picks and chooses its neighbors out of self-concern, it does not draw the lines of inclusion and exclusion as to the object of its concerns out of prejudice for our kind of neighbor. Christian justice treats equal cases equally.

Yet no concrete choice among competing neighbor claims is an exact equality of claims and rights. We must recognize the third quality of Christian justice as the indirect expression of love: *proportional* justice, or the unequal distribution of goods, proportionate to the differing levels of merit, need, age, accomplishment. In the eyes of agape, every neighbor is special, exceptional. To treat dissimilar cases similarly, with a mechanical equity, would be grossly unjust. Proportional justice, then, grounded in the loving regard for each neighbor as different, poses vexing problems for conscientious choice. Yet it stands as a normative principle to guide choices amid the welter of colliding values and needs that require decision and action. Should a parent discipline a teenager as severely as a seven-year-old child? Obviously, the variant of greater maturity of one child should make the discipline imposed sensitive to the difference in age. In giving grades in a college course, I would hardly be just in giving every student a B-minus, regardless of the quality of the work done in the course. In the larger circles of public policy, the variables are compounded enormously. For the Internal Revenue Service, in the name of equity, to exact a flat income tax of $4,000 from every citizen, no matter the level of income, would be a gross injustice. Thus proportional justice in our steeply graded income tax policy (at least theoretically) taxes the wealthy more than the poor, though the norm of equality is also present in a tax policy that demands roughly equal revenue from everyone in the same income bracket. When the terms of a labor contract are set, the variables of need, seniority, tenure, quality of workmanship, profit of the management, and the prospective security of the industry itself have to be weighed in the balance. No labor contract can do full justice to all these variables, but a "rough justice" should be sensitive to the legitimate needs and demands voiced from both sides of the bargaining table. Our penal system starts from the baseline of equal justice for all, but any particular court decision must take into account the vast range of complex and unequal factors of age, culpability, merit, need, past records of criminal activity, to render a decision that approximates a rough justice.

One of the currents running strong in current Christian ethical theory is the movement known as liberation theology.[6] Liberation theologians cry out in the name of the Hebrew prophets and of Christ for the victims of past and present oppression—racial, generic, economic, national—and for radical systemic changes in our social and economic order to redress the inequities of past exploitation by giving special advantages to the downtrodden, the disenfranchised, the oppressed. Reverse discrimination for minority groups may result in the exclusion of some of the privileged majorities, who may have superior qualifications, from admission to schools or jobs. It is protested that such policies contradict the norm of equality. Yet, liberation theologians would defend such inequalities in the name of Christian justice.

The ethical rationale for such inequality in administering justice is, again, to be found in the distinctive quality of agape, for such love is sensitive to the fact that every person or group of persons is exceptional, deviant from the baseline of equality, and therefore deserves exceptional treatment. If justice as equality is grounded in the parity of all creatures, justice as inequality is grounded in the complex heritage of inequalities in merit, need, and status, which obtain in every matrix of choice. This justice is called proportional justice.

In this love-justice dialectic, I have attempted to show the positive connection of Christian love with justice: the impartiality of justice resting upon love's disinterestedness, the equality of justice resting upon love's regard for the equal worth of all persons, the proportionality of justice resting on the inequalities of merit and need that should be honored. And these qualities of a loving justice are grounded and validated by the Christian theological faith-premises (Level V) as to the way God creates, governs, and redeems the human community. Yet, withal—and this is the negative side of the dialectic—distance and tension remain between what agape requires and what any particular policy of justice, however conscientious and careful, can realize. For policy in public affairs, whether in business or educational administration, in politics, in legislative, executive, or judicial, or international affairs, however sensitive it may try to be to the complexity of variants, must necessarily treat persons as cases in this or that bracket. In public policy, persons become "its" not "Thou's," to use Martin Buber's distinction between "I-Thou" and "I-it." No particular public policy can ever do full justice to the mandate of the great commandment.

This tension and distance need not lead us to the cynical conclusion that pragmatism is the norm for justice or that if all moral choices are morally ambiguous, "anything goes." No. That would lead to the ethics of the "operator" and to moral anomie. It means only that life's real choices are inevitably compromises. The choice between the absolute best and the absolute worst is foreclosed by the context: we have to choose between the better and the worse. But integrity and compromise are not necessarily opposed to each other. The integrity of the Christian life does not mean a purity of innocence; it means a consistent and conscientious will to choose the relatively better over the relatively worse, which means the highest attainable quality of life for the greatest number of persons. Here is the absolute divine imperative, the righteousness that seeks as the fruit of its faith to "do justly, to love mercy, and to walk humbly."

Part II
Christian Ethics in Practice

6

Sexuality, Marriage, and Christian Love

Now, to apply the Christian ethical norms spelled out in the preceding chapters to particular concrete issues. This section is designed to move outward in a series of concentric circles from the most intimate problems to the larger circles of systems and structures, economic and political.

The first pressing concern is sexual relationships. No college or seminary student involved in a romance of whatever degree of intensity, from casual dating to engagement, needs to be told that the problems of ethical choice here are worrisome. And the problems are by no means solved for good and all at the altar, where a marriage is formally solemnized. Responsible decisions have to be made within the larger context of the revolution in American culture during this century in the pattern of family life, one that challenges the traditional nuclear family unit as the established norm.

Several factual aspects of the cultural context affect moral decision. Using the pattern of double contextualism—the context of faith and the context of facts—outlined in chapter 5, recall first some crucial empirical facts. For one, technology has made available a wide variety of birth control devices, notably the pill, which enable a couple to have sexual intercourse with little likelihood of pregnancy. The pill and other contraceptive devices are readily available, almost "over the counter." And now, with the dire spread of AIDS, condoms are available at college and university stores as well as at health clinics. Even so, the rate of teenage pregnancy has markedly increased, especially among poor and black minorities.[1] Not surprisingly, Kinsey's surveys of some decades ago and more recent studies show that among college and university students 76% of the men and 59% of the women have had sexual relations. Of those polled, 50% of the men and 47% of the women felt no guilt or regret.[2] Another study revealed that of the brides who currently stand before the altar to take the solemn vows of matrimony, one out of six is pregnant. Another factor is the changed pattern of living arrangements on almost all campuses. Men's colleges and women's colleges are now few and far between, an endangered species. Most campuses are co-ed; dormitories are increasingly co-ed. And even at a few such quaint rites as fraternity or sorority dances, who has recently seen chaperones present to monitor behavior? There may be a few futile attempts at retaining a Puritan ethic: at Bob Jones University, students are not allowed to hold hands on campus, at least publicly, and at Liberty Baptist College in Virginia, only double-dating is permitted to freshmen and sophomores. But these are hardly prevailing campus practices.

The Changing Family Pattern in American Culture

Another important sociological fact is a drastic change in the nature and function of the monogamous family unit in American society. On the surface, it appears sure and secure: 96% of Americans marry. But underneath that surface appearance, the institution itself is insecure. The most startling index of this is the rapid rise in the rate of divorce. In 1870, one of thirty-seven marriages ended in divorce. In 1960, one of four. Currently, one of two. This means that four of ten children of divorced couples will be brought up in single-parent households. And even when divorced persons marry someone else, as some 75% do, when children are involved, stepparenting brings difficult tensions and adjustments, for instance, in custody rulings. And for the children, the potential split of affections between a natural parent and a stepparent is often traumatic.

Many causes lie behind the radical change in the American family pattern. Although we should not picture the American home of a century ago as a Norman Rockwell painting, the sociological data surely confirm the generalization that the American family today is hardly the close, congenial unit pictured on TV commercials. In the first place, the family has moved from the farm to the city or to suburbia. On the farm, where most Americans lived a century ago, it was an economic asset to have a large family, for all members, children included, worked together. In the city or in the suburb, the large family is an economic liability. Moreover, in the lifestyle of our industrial urban culture, there are more forces that pull the family apart than pull them together. A century or so ago, the education, work, and recreation of the family was done largely on the farm, together, at home. Now, Dad goes to the office to work. Nearly 50% of mothers are in the work force, at least part-time, away from home. The urban standard of living and the expense of education require more and more that both parents be employed to make ends meet. Currently, in fewer than one-third of two-parent families is the husband the sole breadwinner. And with the sharp increase in single-parent households, in which the mother normally has custody of children, who will take care of them if she has to find a job to make ends meet? If she is one of the many thousands of teenagers with a baby but no husband, how can she go back to school to learn the skills to qualify her for a job?

No longer a function of the home, education is carried on at school and at an earlier and earlier age, in kindergartens and day-care centers. Recreation and play take place away from home with one's peers: soccer, basketball, swimming for the teenagers, Dad on the golf course, Mom at her aerobics class. Even when a family is together, watching TV, the recreation is done for us from outside. We are not playing together. Home seems to have become a place we go through on the way to somewhere else.[3]

A century ago the elderly and the sick were cared for at home; now Grandma is in a retirement home, and the infirm are cared for in the hospital. The number of extended families, three generations living in one household, has sharply declined.

These forces and factors serve more to disintegrate than to unite the family unit.

The Celebration of Sex

A factor that further compounds the problem of moral choice in sex and marriage is the celebration of sex. Through advertising we are constantly bombarded with aphrodisiacs. Cars, shampoos, toothpastes, cold cereals, pizzas—practically everything—are marketed on the basis of their sex appeal. The ad showing the luscious blonde leaning over the fender of the newest model car conveys subliminally the expectation that she is one of the accessories that comes with the car. This is a sly and delicate form of pornography. A more open and raw form of pornography appears on magazine racks, in the movies, and on TV. Our culture is so saturated with sex that our youngsters quickly adopt a mind-set that the essential bond between male and female is physical, not spiritual. Is it any wonder, given this form of sex education, that intimate sexual activity on campus is so common?

Christian Ethical Norms

Let us turn from the descriptive levels to the normative, from the "is" to the "ought," to explore the relevance of the norms of love and justice to the problems of decision and choice. We should set aside at once the ascetic prejudice still held by many devout church folk, who view all sex with suspicion and regard sexual activity as to be engaged in only warily and minimally to assure the continuation of the race. To be sure, *The Joy of Sex* would not likely have been found in the library of the Pilgrim colony at Massachusetts Bay. Even today more than a few in a congregation would be disturbed by the text of a hymn in a new Canadian Episcopal hymnal:

> Now thank we God for bodies strong, vitality and zest,
> For strength to meet the day's demands,
> The urge to give our best,
> For all the body's appetites which can fulfillment find,
> And for the sacrament of sex that recreates our kind.[4]

In contrast to this lingering ascetic tradition, the basic affirmation of the Christian faith is that sex (or to use the polite euphemism, "sexuality") is a created good. Sexual passion is a good part of our natures, to be received with gratitude, indeed a sacrament. Sex is a part of the given order of God's creation that human beings share with all forms of animal life—the birds of the air and the beasts of the field. But there is a crucial difference between human beings and rabbits. Among persons, *sex* is a relational term, obviously in a physical sense, but more importantly in a psychological and a spiritual sense. Sex finds its true worth within a certain kind of personal relationship, and the morality of sexual relations, normatively speaking, depends on the spiritual context of the ends in which it is practiced: the context of love.

Love between a man and a woman can be understood at three levels:

In a purely physiological sense, love as libido means sexual passion. The act of sexual intercourse in a purely physical sense involves the insertion of the male penis into the lubricated vagina of a woman. If all goes well, an orgasm is realized, a highly pleasurable sensation, like a sneeze *in excelsis*. In a purely physical sense this is what a man may experience with a prostitute. But what makes the sexual relationship in a loving marriage different is a psychological, spiritual quality in the transaction. It is an expression of affection, not lust.

Love in the second sense means *philia*, or friendship, an affinity of likes and dislikes, the compatibility of a man and a woman who fit well together in their personalities and lifestyles. *Philia* as affinity does not necessarily mean identity, that Susan is just a photocopy of Bob. They may have separate persuasions, talents, and recreations, but at the same time they are congenial, meshing well in their life together.

Love in the third sense is agape, as defined earlier. In a happy marriage, agape means a lifelong trust in and commitment to the other in a faithful partnership. It involves tenderness, forgiveness, patience, forbearance, the sacrifice of one's own interests for the good of one's spouse. Agape is the moral basis of the Judeo-Christian affirmation of the worth of monogamy, as opposed to polygamy or polyandry.

All three levels of love—*libido, philia, agape*—are present in a Christian view of the "holy estate of matrimony." However, a vital marriage is not really a state. It is a process, a continual growth through periods of stress and trial, "in plenty and in want, for better, for worse." In that process, the bond of a maturing marriage becomes less libidinal and more and more one of *philia* and agape. If the bond is only a physical one, the marriage may become a contest of competing egos and is likely to strain or break apart.[5]

Christian Love in Sexual Practice

How does this three-faceted norm of Christian love relate to Christian decision in sexual practice? It follows from what has been said about the relationship of sex to love and from the norm of Christian monogamy that nonmarital sex, or recreational sex, as it is called, is wrong, for the relationship is purely physical, with no commitment to or responsibility for the other person. It is the use of another's body for self-satisfaction. The sin here is not in the body, but in the will. Lust is the misuse of a good body by a bad will. Note that the same sin may appear within a formalized marriage, for example, when a husband dominates his wife for his own sexual satisfaction—a form of rape.

*Extra*marital sex, an affair with someone other than one's spouse, violates the covenant bond of loyalty and fidelity. It brings with it the dark suspicions and tensions that lead to a troubled or broken marriage. Here again, the sin in adultery is to be located in the will, in infidelity, in breaking faith, not in the body.

When it comes to the question of *pre*marital sexual relations, the morality of the matter becomes more ambiguous. Currently, the context is often one in which the couple at the upper levels of their education have long since reached their physical sexual maturity (girls now menstruate at the average age of twelve or thirteen), but economic and educational circumstances prevent the sensible possibility of their formal marriage until their educations are completed and they can be employed and make a home. In short, they are old enough to have sex but too young to get married. Yet they may be committed to each other, whether or not they are formally engaged. A bond of philia and agape holds them together. No legalism either proscribing or prescribing premarital relations will suffice here. The morality of the matter depends on the circumstances, on the couple's open, honest mutual understanding of the relationship between sex and love, and their acknowledgment of the risks involved, especially the need for sensible precautions against pregnancy. All in all, it may prove that the most responsible thing to do is to postpone intercourse until they are married.

The Problem of Divorce

As to the rights and wrongs of divorce, we must look underneath the tangle of legal technicalities to the ethical issues within the laws.

The traditional position of both the Roman Catholic church and the Religious Right is that divorce is morally wrong. For the Roman church, marriage is a sacrament, solemnized by the church, and as such is indissoluble. Therefore, those divorced persons who are strict adherents to the Roman faith and who seek a second marriage cannot have that marriage blessed by a priest. To be sure, a Roman Catholic marriage can be annulled if there is sufficient evidence that the circumstances of the marriage were invalid in the first place. Many conservative Protestants are opposed to divorce on the grounds of a biblical prohibition attributed to Jesus (Mark 10:11–12), which says whoever divorces his or her spouse commits adultery.

A more liberal persuasion is to be found in the mainline churches of the Protestant tradition, which, while honoring the sanctity of monogamous marriage, recognizes the reality that marriages do fail. Holy wedlock sometimes becomes unholy deadlock. Divorce is then the most caring action to be taken, for the good of all persons involved. As Martin Luther once put it, "When the grain of understanding and affection is ground away between the upper and nether millstones and the stones grind against each other," it is best to seek a divorce. Sometimes a couple who are estranged and in continual collision will stay together, as they say, "for the sake of the children," not recognizing that the tensions in their household may have a devastating effect on the children. It may in most cases be for the sake of the children that a divorce should be sought.

When the true bonds of a loving marriage, *philia* and agape, have been strained to the breaking point, a divorce is the ethical course, however painful, for it opens up the chance for each person to seek a second marriage and a second home where the bond of love may hold for good.

The legal procedures of divorce come within the jurisdiction of the state, not the church. Yet law and ethics are intertwined in many issues, and the liberalization of laws is needed. Divorce was once an adversary proceeding in which one person was presumed innocent and the other guilty; now no-fault laws in forty-eight states permit divorce on the grounds of mutual separation after a legally fixed period of time. When children are involved, custody and visitation rights often pose difficult ethical quandaries for a judge. But decisions that seek the best possible care of the children, sometimes through shared custody, are increasingly common. Alimony and financial assurance for the education of the children are expressions of proportional justice.

Perhaps the most helpful response of the Christian community—pastors, counselors, teachers, parents—is the practice of preventive medicine, that is, not the prohibition of divorce but a counteroffensive against the centrifugal forces in our society that are destructive of the monogamous family unit, through programs and therapies that will strengthen family bonds of love so that fewer people will seek divorce. Many positive measures exist. Pastoral or marriage counseling can lead those in a troubled marriage to be more open and trustful in spilling their resentments, which in turn may lead to reconciliation. Another is family-centered activities. If our urban industrial culture precludes the family's working together as a unit, as they did on the farm, we can at least learn to play together by turning off the TV and discovering delight in family outings, sports, dance, music making, or the pursuit of other hobbies. The role of a church program in strengthening family ties through worship, recreation, and community service can be a positive centripetal force. As a counteroffensive against the exponential rate of teenage sexual activity and teenage pregnancy, one of the most important things a church can do in its educational program, in cooperation with comparable programs in public schools, is to provide sex education, not just in the physiological facts, but more important in the morality and spirituality of sex, to convey to youth the Christian normative understanding of the relationship of sex and love in responsibility.

Homosexuality

Finally, an issue that the gay liberation movement has brought out of the closet is homosexuality, specifically the morality or immorality of homosexual relationships, gay or lesbian. The scientific evidence runs against the conventional wisdom, strongly held by conservative religious groups, that according to Genesis the fixed order of creation is one of heterosexuality: "God created male and female," or as Jerry Falwell put it, "God created Adam and Eve, not Adam and Steve." If we can set aside this traditional position for a moment and examine the facts that scientists have learned, we discover that all persons in their XYX genetic makeup have homosexual and heterosexual inclinations, especially at the time of puberty. Although the vast majority of persons develop a dominant heterosexual orientation, a minority of persons remain sexually oriented to persons of their own gender. The precise percentage is difficult to determine: perhaps 6% to 8% of males, 2% to 4% of females. Also, some of these homosexually oriented persons are bisexual, inclined toward sexual intercourse with those of either gender. Whether homosexuals are homosexuals because of "nature" or "nurture" is a real puzzle, but scientific evidence seems to lean toward the conclusion that it is more a matter of nature than of nurture. Such study has led the scientific community to regard homosexuality as a deviance from heterosexuality, but—as the American Psychiatric Association recently affirmed—it is not a disorder, any more than left-handedness is a disorder, and it is in no sense morally culpable.

What then should be a normative Christian response to a gay or a lesbian? Certainly values are in collision here. The sanctity of the man-woman relationship in a monogamous family, for the expression of love and the procreation of children, seems to conflict with the societal good of a homosexual relationship. Yet conflicting with that value is the Christian regard for the dignity and worth of all persons, especially the oppressed and the victims of prejudice.

As gays and lesbians have come out more and more publicly, as Gay Alliances have appeared on more and more campuses, and as "metropolitan churches" (sanctuaries for avowed gays and lesbians who feel ostracized from their own churches) have formed in more and more cities, the responses of official Christian church bodies have been mixed and uncertain. Reactions range from outright condemnation and rejection, through a cautious moderate position that honors and respects the sacred worth of all homosexual persons and protects their civil rights but also does not condone homosexual practice,[6] to a liberal position that assesses the morality of homosexual relations and heterosexual relations by the same criterion. That is, the Christian qualities of love are agape and *philia*, and these qualities may be as present in a gay or lesbian marriage as in a heterosexual marriage. As one scholar put it, "In actuality, compared with heterosexual couples, committed gay couples show no intrinsic or qualitative differences in their capacities for self-giving love."[7] The line of moral distinction between right and wrong here, in other words, is not to be drawn by the physiological difference between a relationship between "straights," which is by definition good, and between gays, which is intrinsically bad. No, the moral line to be drawn is the spiritual difference between a covenanted relationship of mutual love and a loveless or an exploitative relationship. The moral difference is in the will, not the body.

This liberal persuasion leads Christian communities to respect gays and lesbians and welcome them in their circle, to offer facilities for meetings of Gay Alliance groups, to arrange forums for dialogue between straights and gays. Should homosexuals be eligible for ordination as pastors of Christian churches? A person of conservative religious persuasion would say no, for the pastor of a church, whether man or woman, should be a role model for the congregation, a loving spouse, or, if single, a celibate. Yet the same moral logic behind the liberal position that would accept fully an avowed practicing homosexual into the community of the church would favor ordination of a homosexual who meets all the traditional qualifications for the ministry. Indeed, the suspicion, ostracism, and scorn that a homosexual has suffered might deepen his or her sensitivity in ministry and counseling. It is, again, the quality of sympathetic love, not sexual orientation, that becomes the significant criterion.

The moral dilemmas of the rights and wrongs of homosexuality have been tragically intensified by the recent plague of AIDS (acquired immune deficiency syndrome). Although brought to public attention only as recently as the early 1980s, this fatal disease has spread in America like the bubonic plague of the fourteenth century, though not at the horrendous rate that it has spread in Africa. By August 1987, the death toll in America was conservatively estimated at more than twenty-two thousand persons, and one and a half million more Americans are thought to be infected with the AIDS virus. Intensive medical research has yet to produce preventive measures or sure cures.[8]

The vast majority of those afflicted are male homosexuals and hard-drug addicts who become infected through contaminated needles. These persons have made up 90% of the known casualties, though the data are difficult to ascertain. Hemophiliacs are also highly susceptible. Although the rate of spread among homosexuals has been lowered somewhat, the number of drug-abusing heterosexual persons infected with AIDS is on the rise. Although the largest number of AIDS cases has been documented in the depressed areas of metropolitan centers such as New York City and San Francisco, the disease is moving throughout the country.

The horror is deepened by the fact that the infants born of

those who carry the AIDS virus may be also infected with HIV, the human immunodeficiency virus, which is potentially deadly. It was estimated that in 1987 some 1,000 HIV-infected babies were born in New York City, nearly all of them to women who were on hard drugs or whose sexual partners were drug abusers. What can be done? Until medical science can discover an effective cure, some preventive measures may help to check the spread of AIDS.

Sex education programs, in churches as well as in schools, can alert all persons, especially youngsters, not only to the medical facts but also to the values at stake and to responsible behavior. People should learn that casual sexual encounters greatly increase the chance of infection and that the use of hard drugs is a destructive addiction in itself, quite apart from the peril of contracting AIDS through contaminated needles. The wisest precautionary measure for persons other than heterosexual married couples is to abstain from full sexual relations.

Thus far the scientific evidence does not indicate that one can become infected through everyday contacts at the office, at home, or at school. Almost always, it is only through sexual contact or by using infected needles that the deadly virus is spread.

Some alarmed citizens have proposed that school systems exclude the children who have the AIDS virus. In some states, legislation has been proposed to mandate blood tests for couples applying for marriage licenses, for prison inmates, or for illegal aliens seeking amnesty. Such proposals go too far and would avail little to check the spread of the epidemic. Moreover, such laws would run counter to the Fourth Amendment of the Constitution, which protects "the right of the people to be secure in their persons, houses, papers, and effects, against unreasonable searches and seizures." No, until medical science can come up with a cure, the normative prescriptive check against the spread of this disease must come from within by arousing the consciences of all to responsible behavior, to abstention from all casual sexual relations, for the protection of our own lives and the lives of our children. [9]

7

Birthing and Dying

We come now to the troublesome and morally ambiguous issues of bioethics, the life-and-death options in which everyone— those who make personal, private decisions, those who determine law and public policy, as well as those who practice medicine— confronts dilemmas that defy simple solutions.

One of the most hotly debated issues is the morality of abortion. In recent years we have seen a sharp polarization of conviction between the proponents and the opponents of abortion. Indeed, a few opponents of abortion are so militant as to plant bombs in Planned Parenthood and other clinics where abortions are performed, in the name of the right to life, endangering the lives of those who work at these clinics. At the moment, we seem to be a house divided: pro-choice against pro-life.

The Empirical Context

Many factors in the context of this debate—sociological, demographic, technological, ecological, political—need to be weighed in the moral equation of private decision and public policy. One major factor, of course, is the population explosion. On a worldwide scale, despite stringent efforts by some nations such as the People's Republic of China to limit the rate of population growth, the world's population grows exponentially while the resources of the earth to sustain this growth are progressively exhausted. In global terms, if the present rate of growth continues, in twenty-five years two persons will stand where one stands now. In the United States, the birth rate has stabilized, with minor fluctuations, at just under 2.0; that is, the median number of children born into American families is approximately two. However, with the developments in health care and medicine in this century, the life span of the average American has been extended from forty to more than seventy. And with the continuing waves of immigration, especially of Hispanics, the population in America continues to grow—thirteen million more persons in 1985 than in 1970. There is a growing gap between the rich, who tend to have fewer children, and the poor, who tend to have more. Birth control by some means or other becomes a moral imperative to limit population if the human race is to survive.[1] The use of contraceptives is the readiest way to limit birth rate, more humane than sterilization and vasectomy. Yet abortion after conception is an alternative way of birth control.

One important technological development is improved abortion procedures, which do not endanger the life of the woman or cancel the possibility of successful later birthing. Of course, abortion has been practiced for at least four thousand years, but earlier methods were crude and dangerous. Another important technological advance in medical science, amniocentesis, which is performed during the middle trimester of pregnancy, can detect such genetic abnormalities as Down's syndrome or spina bifida, a severe deformity of the spinal cord. It also detects the gender of the fetus. A more recent technique called "chorionic villus biopsy" can detect abnormalities much earlier in pregnancy. Other techniques can save the life of an infant who weighs as little as two to three pounds at birth.

The problem of choice is seriously compounded by the question, when does the fetus become a human person, in the sense of becoming a living soul? All sorts of conflicting answers are heard. Some say, at the moment of conception, when sperm and egg are joined. (This would seem to make the use of the morning-after pill or the IUD an act of abortion rather than contraception.) Those of the older Roman Catholic tradition say that "ensoulment" takes place at the time of quickening. For Thomas Aquinas, who took his cue from Aristotle, the quickening of a male fetus takes place forty days after conception; of a female fetus, ninety days. Still others say the fetus becomes a person when the fetus becomes viable (usually after seven months). And still others say, at birth. This question cannot be answered in chronological terms, whether by medical scientists or by lawyers (as the 1973 *Roe v. Wade* decision and subsequent rulings of the courts have conceded) or by theologians. It would be impossible to decree that until October 30 at 9:05 A.M., one fetus is but a bit of organic tissue in the pregnant woman's body, then at 9:06 A.M. that fetus becomes a living person with sacred and inviolable rights. The most one can say, perhaps, is that the fetus is potentially a person.

Still another factor that affects the morality of abortion choice has to do with the circumstances of conception. Was the fetus conceived by rape or by incest? Is the life of the mother at peril?

Moral Norms: Pros and Cons

As noted, the current debate on abortion is a standoff between pro-life advocates, who oppose any and all abortions on the grounds of the sanctity of life from the moment of conception, and the pro-choice advocates, who assert a woman's absolute right of choice over her own body. So one sees pro-lifers carrying signs such as "Abortion is Murder" but elsewhere women carrying slogans such as "Abortion is a Woman's Right" or "Keep your hands off my body." Those of the Christian faith are sharply divided. The Roman Catholic church, as expressed in papal encyclicals such as Pope Paul VI's *Humanae Vitae* (1968), opposes both artificial contraception and "directly willed or procured abortion, even if for therapeutic reasons . . . as licit means of regulating birth." The Religious Right is equally adamant in opposition: life is sacred; no human being should take another's life. Curiously, however, the Religious Right favors capital punishment. Their reply to this seeming inconsistency is to distinguish between the innocent life of the fetus, which should be protected, and the protection of society against heinous crimes of murder, which warrant retributive justice.

Yet the right to life versus the right to choose is not the most significant value conflict at stake here. Debated in this form, it is likely to remain a stalemate. At a deeper level, the real value conflict is between the value of life per se, measured in a purely physiological sense, and the quality of life that is likely for the child and for those who would be responsible for his or her care. Would not the future of an infant born with a severe case of Down's syndrome or another serious abnormality augur a sub-human existence for that child and spell "murder" in a spiritual sense, or at least prolonged suffering and agony for the mother and those who care for the child? And if the medical judgment is that the pregnant woman's life is at high risk, the option is to save one life or another life, to which the simple pro-life motto can give no answer.

But who should have the rightful power of choice in such tight dilemmas? Here again, rights seem to collide. If a pregnant woman seeks an abortion because childbearing would be an inconvenience to her in pursuing her career or if amniocentesis reveals that the fetus is female and she and her husband want a male child, an abortion could hardly be deemed a responsible choice. Should it then be the province of the state to decide the legitimacy of abortion? Measures such as the Hyde amendment, introduced in Congress to prohibit the use of federal funds for abortion except to save the life of a pregnant woman, would limit private choice. Or should the decision be made by the pediatrician, who could assess the laboratory evidence as to how severely deformed the fetus might be?

Christian Normative Guidelines

The basic ethical norm that should guide decisions here is derived from agape, translated into a caring proportional justice, i.e., policies and practices that would seek the highest possible quality of life for all the persons involved in the tight dilemma of choice.

A responsible normative answer would be that the decision about abortion should be made corporately by the potential parents, by the attending physicians, and by the officials who regulate public policy. In many hospitals, committees made up of doctors, ethicists, chaplains, and counselors provide prudent corporate judgments in particular cases.

The Roman Catholic church and the Religious Right are vigorously opposed to abortion; the mainline Protestant churches and the Reformed Jewish faith have in their statements of social policy supported the moral legitimacy of abortion under certain circumstances. The Religious Coalition for Abortion Rights is made up of various commissions on public policy from the Reformed Jewish faith, Protestant churches such as American Baptist, Disciples of Christ, the Episcopal, Lutheran, Presbyterian, Mormon, United Church of Christ, United Methodist, American Friends Service Committee, and other church groups. The statement of the United Methodist Church is typical of the liberal position:

> When an unacceptable pregnancy occurs, a family, and most of all the pregnant woman is confronted with . . . a difficult decision. We believe that continuance of a pregnancy which endangers the life or health of the mother, or poses other serious problems concerning the life, health, or mental capability of the child to be, is not a moral necessity. In such a case, we believe the path of mature Christian judgment may indicate the advisability of abortion.[2]

The Presbyterian Church, U.S., took a similar position:

> The willful termination of pregnancy by medical means on the considered decision of a pregnant woman may on occasion be morally justifiable. Possible justifying circumstances would include medical indications of physical or mental deformity, conception as a result of rape or incest, conditions under which the physical or mental health of either mother or child would be gravely threatened, or the socio-economic conditions of the family.[3]

These and comparable statements acknowledge that an abortion is a difficult and, indeed, traumatic action. Yet, using the norm of Christian agape, as a caring concern, translated into a justice that seeks the highest possible quality of life for the widest possible range of persons, I concur with "A Call to Concern," issued some years ago by a group of Christian theologians: "Considering the best medical advice, the best moral insight, and a concern for the total quality of the whole life cycle of the born and the unborn, we believe that abortion may in some instances be the most loving act possible."[4]

Such conscientious statements by church bodies and moral theologians were made in defense of the *Roe v. Wade* decision of the Supreme Court in 1973. Though pro-life advocates now regard *Roe v. Wade* as an outrageously wrong decision, the decision itself is a cautious compromise between free choice and state regulation. Note its actual terms:

> For the stage prior to approximately the end of the first trimester, the abortion decision and its effectuation must be left to the medical judgment of the pregnant woman's attending physician. For the stage subsequent to approximately the end of the first trimester, the State, in promoting its interest in the health of the mother, may, if it chooses, regulate the abortion procedure in ways that are reasonably related to maternal health.
> [During the last ten weeks, however, when the fetus is considered viable,] the State in promoting its interests in the potentiality of human life may, if it chooses, regulate, and even proscribe, abortion except where it is necessary . . . for the life or health of the mother.[5]

This balanced but generally liberal ruling of the Supreme Court has been somewhat qualified by a ruling of 1977, which held that the states are not obliged to use public funds such as Medicaid for abortions for poor women or to offer elective nontherapeutic abortions for free. Despite increasing fire from the militant pro-life advocates, *Roe v. Wade* still stands as the law of the land and was reaffirmed by the Supreme Court in June 1986, although by a narrower margin of votes than in 1973.

New Technologies of Reproduction

Another aspect of the birthing process takes us into an area of recent sophisticated medical technology—artificial techniques to achieve pregnancy and birth—that poses unprecedented ethical problems. Although to a university or seminary student these issues may not seem immediately urgent, it will not be long (given the rapidity with which scientific technologies are being perfected) before they will be knocking at the doors of decision.

When a married couple who want to have children are for reasons of sexual impotence or sterility incapable of achieving pregnancy through the normal process of intercourse, artificial means now can produce pregnancy. One procedure (called AIH, artificial-insemination-husband) is to use instruments to inject the husband's semen into the wife's vagina. Another (AID, artificial-insemination-donor) is to insert the semen from a man other than the husband into the woman's vagina. Though still a tiny ratio of the total population, well over twenty-five thousand Americans now living were conceived by either AIH or AID.[6] In still another method (IVF, in vitro fertilization) the male sperm is joined with the female egg in a test tube. If the egg becomes fertilized, it is inserted in the woman's uterus; if the implantation is successful, the pregnancy is begun. In a variation of the IVF procedure, the sperm or egg is from a third person. Surrogate mothers, under the terms of a legal contract, may either receive a woman's fertilized ovum or be artificially inseminated with the partner's sperm. The surrogate mother carries the fetus to term, and the baby is then returned to the first woman.

As one moves across the spectrum from AIH to surrogate mothers, the morality of the procedure becomes much more problematic. Some conservative Christian ethicists rule out AID as a subtle form of adultery, though that classification is questionable, since adultery means infidelity in the act of sexual relation with a person other than one's spouse, and in AID there is no such infidelity. All things considered, I affirm artificial insemination and in vitro fertilization as morally legitimate ways for naturally infertile couples to realize one of the rich blessings of a marriage: to have children. As for surrogate motherhood, as the "Baby M" case brought to public attention in 1987, the psychological and moral problems of that triangular relationship may prove so complex and perilous that a couple would be better advised to seek adoption through an adoption agency, slow and difficult as that process is. There may certainly be cases in which the adoptive parents maintain a close and happy relationship with the child's birth-mother.

Euthanasia

At the other end of the life line is death, inevitable sooner or later for everyone. Yet, like the ethical problems of birthing, ethical dilemmas also arise in dealing with how persons die, problems that have been created by the radical changes in medical technology, as well as in the cultural context of American life. In our century, vaccines and inoculations have eliminated many of the devastating plagues—malaria, polio, and tuberculosis—that crippled or killed millions. In this century, too, medical technology has prolonged the expected life span of Americans by forty or more years. An increasing proportion of our population are senior citizens, in their seventies or eighties, with serious or minor ailments of all sorts. Sometimes the ethical dilemmas strike at a much earlier age. One was brought to national attention in the case of Karen Ann Quinlan, the twenty-one-year-old victim of an overdose of drugs who fell into a comatose "permanent vegetative state" but was not allowed by court decision to die, despite the pleas of her parents, backed by their Catholic priest, and so remained "alive" for more than ten years even after the artificial respirator was removed. The Quinlan case is by no means unique.

A medical issue compounds the problem. Contrary to conventional wisdom, which regards death as a specific moment when life ceases, death in medical terms is a gradual process, a sequence of stages: "clinical" death, when vital functions of heartbeat and breathing cease; "brain" death; "biological" death, and finally; "cellular" death. In current medical and legal practice, brain death, as measured by a flat EEG (electroencephalogram), is accepted as the stage at which a person is officially dead. The ethical problem is that technical machineries of various sorts, such as respirators, can now keep a person "alive" in the earlier stages of dying. But a physician is bound by the Hippocratic Oath: "to help the sick, never with a view to injury and wrong-doing." A conservative reading of that oath implies that the doctor is obliged to do everything possible to preserve life. A liberal reading would mean that the doctor should "help the sick" by allowing the patient in acute pain and suffering from a terminal illness to die. The answers, however, are neither simple nor easy to reach.

The Fading of the Doctrine of Immortality

Another significant change has occurred in the cultural context in which we view the life-and-death sequence. For earlier Western cultures, in which the Christian doctrine about the human story prevailed, this life was viewed as a fleeting episode in the pilgrimage of the soul, going through this life to life beyond. This doctrine was based on the assurance of St. Paul, in his letter to the Corinthians and in other places, "We know that if the earthly tent we live in is destroyed, we have a building from God, a house not made with hands, eternal in the heavens" (2 Cor. 5:1). The promise of immortality, when "this perishable nature must put on the imperishable, and this mortal nature must put on immortality" (1 Cor. 15:53), gave to those of Christian faith a blessed assurance of immortality beyond this vale of tears. Death then was not the great enemy; it might be indeed a friend, the "saints' everlasting rest," a heavenly home beyond this life. *Komm Süsser Tod* ("Come, Sweet Death").

The belief in the heavenly life beyond this vale of tears is deeply entrenched in the classical Christian tradition and based on more than the words of St. Paul. The whole worldview in the faith-premise of orthodoxy, both Catholic and Protestant, assumed the frail transiency of mortal life and the promise of a life eternal in God, once a person had passed through the gates of death.

In our liturgy we still repeat phrases affirming this belief in immortality, as in the Apostles' Creed, believing "in the resurrection of the body and the life everlasting," or we sing fervently of the heaven promised in the closing stanza of evangelical hymns. At funeral services, Christians are assured of the victory over death in the blessed life to come. However, our general cultural context has become so secularized that the prevailing axiom is that this life is all there is. Beyond this life is oblivion, an abyss. So death becomes the great enemy. Just as heaven as a place "up there" has disappeared from our cosmology (no astronauts, after all, have located it), so immortality is disappearing from our understanding of human destiny. This vast cultural change has had a subtle but profound effect on decisions about the dying process.

The Moral Costs of Life-Sustaining Technologies

Still another troublesome problem has to do with the allocation of scarce resources in the maintenance of human life. Since 1967, when Dr. Christiaan Barnard in South Africa performed the first human heart transplant, the number of such operations has increased steadily, with a very mixed record of success. So, too, has the number of kidney transplants. More recently, artificial hearts have been implanted. Kidney dialysis machines can postpone or prevent death from kidney failure, although the total cost for all machines used in the country comes to nearly two billion dollars a year.[7] Research and experimentation in other very sophisticated technologies to sustain life are being conducted at medical centers. All are very costly. The expense must be borne by the family, by the patient, or by the public. But within an economy of scarcity, the allocation of resources requires some tight preferential choices. William Schroeder's artificial heart, the machinery needed to pump it, and the several strokes that followed the implantation held him at the precipice of death for 620 days, at an exorbitant expense. Might not the thousands and thousands of dollars it cost to maintain his life have been more humanely spent for hunger relief or birth control clinics in Africa? The value of minimal health care for the many collides with the value of keeping one person alive.

In light of all that has been said, if we translate the norm of Christian love as care for persons into a social policy in medical practice that seeks the widest possible concern for all persons involved, it becomes clear that euthanasia, a practice that allows a terminally ill patient in insufferable pain to die, is the most loving action to take.

Euthanasia is of two sorts: passive or active. In passive euthanasia, no "extraordinary" or "heroic" measures are used, or machineries are withdrawn in order to allow death to take its course. The patient is allowed to die in peace. A recent policy ruling of the American Medical Association affirms that a doctor who approves this form of euthanasia does not violate the Hippocratic Oath. In active euthanasia, death is induced by giving the patient a lethal dose of morphine or some other drug. Though some ethicists would say that both active and passive euthanasia are morally justified because the intent in both forms is the same—to bring the blessing of death—the Christian moral preference would be for passive rather than active euthanasia: passive euthanasia allows nature to take its course; active euthanasia requires human intervention.

Who should decide? Preferably, of course, the doctor, in concurrence with the patient. But many patients may no longer be capable of deciding. The patient's immediate family members, as well, should be party to the decision. One practice that is coming into increasing use and that has legal standing in many states is the Living Will, a statement that may be signed by a single person or a married couple, declaring that "I, _____, being of sound mind, willfully or voluntarily make known my desire that my dying shall not be artificially prolonged" and that artificial "life-sustaining procedures be withheld or withdrawn." The Living Will can protect the family of a terminally ill patient from the pain of decision about a beloved family member who is no longer able to decide and for whom all hope of recovery is gone.

Finally, the question as to *where* one dies is of moral moment. Until fairly recently, most people died at home. Now they die in hospitals or nursing homes, within the cold environs of impersonal machineries and among strangers. A morally significant movement that has gained momentum lately is the hospice movement, which now has some 1,700 chapters across the land. Hospice provides adequate nursing and medical care for the terminally ill but allows them to die with dignity, within the familiar and intimate circle of the family, at home. Here is another expression of Christian love and compassion as a caring concern for the whole person, body and soul, which should surround and sanctify the whole life sequence, from birth to death.

This discussion of abortion, euthanasia, and artificial insemination may seem to give disproportionate attention to the descriptive context of medical choice and too little to ethical norms. You might be led to conclude that medical technology becomes the judge of right and wrong. It would be as though to say, "If we have the technology to do something, we ought to do it." This is an example of how pervasive the religion of scientism has become in our secular society and how far we have shifted from a theocratic to a technocratic culture.

To correct the seeming imbalance of emphasis in this chapter, remember that technology is not the arbiter of moral choice. No, the normative guide for Christian decision in medical practices and policy, as in all others, is the norm of responsible love, translated into a caring justice, a care that seeks the highest possible quality of life for all the persons affected by the decision. The hospital, no less than a church, is where Christian love seeks to be obedient and faithful to God's will.

8

Racial and Gender Relations

The ethical issues in human relations among those of different color, gender, or ethnic background are both private and public. They are as close as relations in the home, in the neighborhood, in the schoolyard at recess time. Yet they are also matters of urgent concern in determining public policy and in the enactment and enforcement of state and national laws.

Try to come at this baffling problem by recalling certain basic affirmations of Christian theology from chapter 2, in particular the bottom-line tenet of faith about the given order of creation: unity and diversity. As the Bible puts it: "He made from one every nation of men to dwell on all the face of the earth" (Acts 17:26). Yellow, red, white, black—all stand on a par in God's created order. This faith-premise evokes the response of thanksgiving and gratitude. Black is beautiful. Red is beautiful. White is beautiful. Yellow is beautiful.

Here the Christian faith coincides with the underlying democratic dogma expressed in Jefferson's Declaration of Independence:

"All men are created equal, and . . . are endowed by their Creator with certain inalienable rights."

The divinely set design of equality in creation is the ideal. Alas, we do not live in the order of creation. We live in a fallen order, far east of Eden, where human relations in community are corrupted by sin. In its racial and ethnic form, human sin takes the form of pride, or hubris—those of one skin color or ethnic background take that differential as the criterion of worth. To put the matter theologically, they worship the created, rather than the Creator. Pride becomes, to use Augustine's telling phrase, "a perverse desire of height," the root of prejudice, by which I take my color or ethnic difference as the standard of value. A person of another color then becomes not only different but worse. "White is beautiful" means "Black is not beautiful." Though in our American culture the most evident form of this sin appears in the white-black differential, this same prejudice is strong among Anglo-Saxon farmers in the Dakotas toward Native Americans, among Anglo-Saxon whites in San Francisco and Los Angeles toward Orientals or Hispanics, or among Yankee farmers in Vermont toward French-Canadians, whom they call "Canucks."

The Vicious Circle

The root of the trouble is in the will, since "out of the heart of man are the issues of life." But inward pride and prejudice do not stay confined; they find expressions in the outer systemic structures of education, business, housing, politics. This starts what we might call the vicious circle, which might be diagrammed as follows.

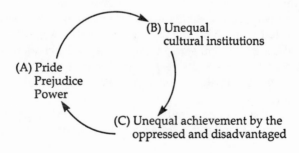

At point A in the circle, people of racial pride and prejudice, holding the reins of power in policy formation, construct institutional walls and structures of segregation (B) to protect their superiority, systems that deny equal opportunity and rights to the oppressed, whether they be minorities or whether they constitute a vast majority, as in South Africa. Then, held under the systems of unequal opportunities in schooling, in job training, the oppressed group cannot achieve at the level of expected excellence (C). In America, for example, the scores on SAT tests of blacks still fall markedly short of those of whites, despite the legal integration of public schools some thirty years ago. And statistics on the crime rate of blacks in the inner city run much higher than that of white citizens. Then C is used to justify the original pride (A) with tangible evidence, to cloak pride in seemingly plausible excuses ("We just can't find qualified blacks"). So we come full circle.

Another trick of the devil in this vicious scenario is called control by stereotype, or group image. The sinful will of human beings deflects the vision of the mind: if I am white, I see the different neighbor, not as a person in depth, but as a "case" of this or that color. I then expect of that person certain traits that I associate with that group image. All other individuating qualities are subsumed or overlooked. For instance, the white group image or stereotype of the black person is that he or she is lazy, given to slovenly speech, murdering the king's English, forever using double negatives and saying "runnin'" or "doin'". These stereotypes are usually negative in comparison to positive white self-images: all white folks are of course inherently industrious and elegant in their speech, never dropping "g's." It is interesting that this group imaging prevails with other ethnic groups. Anglo-Saxons regard Orientals as very polite, feline, sly, and shrewd. Jews are clannish, aggressive, and mercenary, as suggested by the obliquely anti-Semitic bumper sticker "Jesus Saves. Moses Invests." Conversely, blacks have a group image of white persons. "Whitey" is hypocritical, condescending, and nice if you bow to his or her superiority, curt if you stand up for yourself. Most blacks do not trust Whitey to deliver on the equal rights he or she claims to profess.[1]

The walls of segregation are built from the inner walls of pride

and prejudice into systems and structures of housing and schooling and on into the economic structures of manufacturing and
retailing of goods, which retain the power imbalance. They also
keep the oppressed as strangers, at a distance, over there, so that
the group image is confirmed. Those of our race may not know
those of other races as next-door neighbors, because most of them
live in the other community across town.

The tragic strife and warfare that exploded in South Africa in
1986 and 1987, when a white minority elite denied basic economic
and political rights to the black majority, and police killed more
than 1,500 blacks and arrested 36,000 protestors (60% of whom
were under the age of eighteen), evoked a racial civil crisis unlike
anything known in this century. Limits of space prevent my
retelling the long story of race relations in America, except to note
that our own tragic Civil War, between the North and the South in
the mid-nineteenth century, was fought over essentially the same
ethical issue: the emancipation of black slaves, although economic
issues and the tension between states' rights and preserving the
union were also causes of the war. The Emancipation Proclamation reaffirmed, at least in theory, the Christian and democratic
ideal of liberty and justice for all.

But human pride and prejudice continue to block the realization of this goal. Racism was not erased by the Emancipation
Proclamation. The walls of separation have remained high. In the
twentieth century the civil rights movement, under the dynamic
leadership of such persons as Martin Luther King, Jr., and others,
black and white, who spoke for the Christian conscience in the
churches, brought about crucial changes in legislation and in practice. Formal, legal equality was advanced, but the vicious circle still
turned. Racial integration was seen by many blacks as "assimi-
lation"; that is, though blacks were admitted to schools, colleges,
businesses, they were welcomed on white terms and felt that they
were being "whitewashed." In major Protestant seminaries, for
example, even today, some black students resent being educated in
the ways of white worship—formal, cold, without soul—and not
being equipped for the sort of ministries expected in the black
churches to which they will go.

The Black Power movement of the 1950s and 1960s was in part a protest against this unequal form of integration. Its leadership encouraged blacks to go it on their own, building their own banking, commercial, and housing developments, their own schools and colleges, so that at least they could achieve a parity of power, from which a real integration might follow.[2] But attempts to build a self-sufficient black community, such as Soul City, North Carolina, failed largely because of the entrenched white-controlled establishment of the American economic and political systems.

Remember, also, that although the white-black tension is the most visible and troublesome of American racial problems, much of the same vicious circle appears in other ethnic relations, though in less visible and violent forms. The treatment of Native Americans by the white settlers of the nineteenth and twentieth centuries, forcing them to relocate from their native lands into reservations, was a form of white-imposed apartheid. Now a new ethnic tension is boiling up: as Hispanic refugees from Central America are pouring into the country, especially in the Southwest, some classified by the government as illegal aliens, they constitute a threat to the employment and economic security of Caucasian Americans in that area. Their influx is resented and resisted.

The harsh reality is that our interracial practices fall far short of our Christian ethical norms and the democratic credo that we are "one nation, under God, with liberty and justice for all." Whether our racial and ethnic prejudices take a violent or a velvet form, in many tragic ways we experience a broken community of alienation, suspicion, and oppression.

The Christian response to this situation should first of all be one of contrition and repentance before God's judgment, the acknowledgment of our own deep-seated prejudices, however cleverly we hide them from ourselves. If the trouble is rooted in the inner source of will, then social change must spring from a change of heart. This was underscored in the chapters of Part I, the covenantal Christian ethics of response, which answers God's creating beneficence with stewardship, answers God's judgment upon human sin with contrition, and responds to God's forgiving

grace in an ethic of reconciliation, to witness for the original order
of creation, to recover equality of community in the whole human
family.

The Benevolent Circle

An ethic of reconciliation calls for a countermovement against
the vicious circle—a "benevolent circle," which turns in an opposite direction. It might be diagrammed thus:

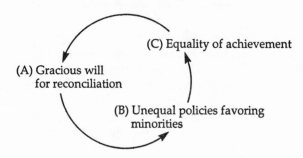

(C) Equality of achievement

(A) Gracious will
for reconciliation

(B) Unequal policies favoring
minorities

The benevolent circle, starting from an inner will (A), emancipated by God's grace from the enslavement of prejudice, will reach
out to support policies and programs that can give particular
benefits and advantages to those whom the vicious circle has
discriminated against in the past. Such programs as Affirmative
Action in employment and Operation Headstart in the schools are
measures of reverse discrimination, yes, but morally justified in
terms of proportional justice, as they begin to redress the inequalities that have victimized minorities for so long. There are serious
ethical and legal problems in such policies. In the famous Bakke
case, in 1978, a white candidate of superior academic qualification
was denied admission to a California medical school, where
enrollment was limited, in favor of a black applicant who had
inferior academic credentials. Bakke protested that he had been
denied the equal protection of the laws and that the admission
policy should be color-blind. Yet the Court's ruling affirmed in
principle the constitutionality of college admissions programs that
give special advantages to blacks and other minorities to help

remedy past discriminations against them (although in this case it did rule in Bakke's favor). The basic ethical principle in this decision, underneath all the technical legalese, is the principle of proportional justice, sensitive to all the variants of need, merit, achievement, and past and present injustices.

In the benevolent circle, pursuit of the unequal policies and practices of proportional justice (B) leads eventually to C: equality of performance and achievement. And C confirms and reassures the trusting steps that the will to reconciliation dared to take. We come full circle to a community restored. The "beloved community" of which Martin Luther King, Jr., dreamed is realized in fact.[3] Here is genuine integration. Another blessing of the reconciled community is that persons are no longer alienated, treating each other as cases, but are brought close, able to know one another's personal qualities and quirks. Interracial relations become interpersonal relations. Persons are freed from the confining walls of pride and prejudice, freed for genuine community. It becomes the moral obligation of the Christian, of whatever color or ethnic background, to follow the course of the benevolent circle, even though it runs counter to the prevailing force of the vicious circle, deeply entrenched in our customs and "habits of heart."

Liberation Theology

Liberation theology, a strong movement in current Christian thought, provides a theological base for much of what I have written about race relations, but its concerns reach far beyond racial or ethnic tensions. The leading spokespersons of the liberation theology movement have been Latin American theologians such as José Míguez Bonino, Gustavo Gutiérrez, and Rubem Alves. They speak in the name of the poor and the oppressed of Latin America and Third World nations who are exploited by the multinational corporations, especially those of the United States. Strongly influenced by the Marxist diagnosis of the inherent cruelty and abusiveness of capitalism, they call for liberation from all the systems of power and privileges that keep the poor down and out, and liberation for a society whose systems of political and economic power will promote reconciliation and equality.

Although the fundamental categories of the Latin American liberation theologians are cast in economic terms, their norms are derived from the prophets of the Old Testament, such as Amos, Hosea, Micah, and Isaiah, who defined the authentic worship of God in terms of justice and righteousness and freedom for those who are poor and oppressed. Their norms are also derived from Jesus himself, in the prophetic tradition, who in a classic parable described the true neighbor to one in need, not as the priest or the Levite, but as the good Samaritan.

The case for liberation theology in the United States has been turned in the direction of racial as well as economic emancipation. Some black theologians, affirming that God is on the side of the oppressed, challenge the imagery of conventional Christianity, which pictures Christ as a white Anglo-Saxon. They would revise the imagery and picture Christ as black.[4] Some of these black theologians press their case so far as to fall into a kind of reverse racism. Rightly, they have ripped the "White Only" signs off the doors leading to Christian community; now they want to put up new signs that read "Black Only." Is this in keeping with the norm of Christian universality and inclusiveness?

The Feminist Movement

Another expression of the liberation theology movement in midcentury has been the feminist movement.[5] No need to rehearse here the long history in Western culture of the masculine domination in family, educational, economic, political, and church life. Biblical imagery is shot through and through with patriarchal idioms: "the Fatherhood of God" and the "Brotherhood of Man." God is King, not Queen, of the universe, Lord, not Lady, over all. The structure of authority in the family has long been patriarchal, one in which women were subordinate to men. Many passages in St. Paul's letters stress this subordinate role, enjoining wives to be obedient to their husbands and to keep silent in church. "If there is anything they desire to know, let them ask their husbands at home. For it is shameful for a woman to speak in church" (1 Cor. 14:35–36).

Until recently, this pattern of male-female relations generally prevailed in the cultures of the West and of the East. The husband has been expected to be the wage earner, the wife the homemaker. In the professions it has been expected that doctors, ministers, lawyers, politicians, and business executives would be men. Women were not given the constitutional right to vote in national elections until the Nineteenth Amendment was passed in 1920, after a long crusade by suffragettes.

By midcentury, advances toward equality of rights and privileges were in evidence: more and more women were pursuing higher education and professional degrees and entering the job market at every level. But the champions of women's lib point out, correctly, that many differentials and inequalities still prevail. The average wage of the working woman is 60% of what a man earns in a comparable position. Most physicians are male; most nurses are female. In the pastoral ministry of churches, a staff of a male pastor and a woman associate pastor is much more common than the reverse. Male chauvinism lingers long in the legal profession, too, and in politics. The old adage still obtains: "A woman's place is in the house, not the Senate."

This established axiom of male chauvinism is reflected in and supported by our conventional sexist language, both secular and religious. When Jefferson wrote that "all men are created equal," he was using the term, of course, in a generic sense, but such language today, at least as heard by militant feminists, is a put-down. To speak of "mankind" or "chairman," or "brotherhood," or "manning the office" may have no chauvinistic intent. Yet it evokes bristles and protests by those committed to women's lib. This poses very awkward problems in liturgy, whose idioms are drenched with masculine imagery. Should a pastor announce: "Let us sing hymn number 564, 'Rise Up, O Men of God'; ladies, please remain seated"?

What shall we do to be saved from these patterns of inequality, unaware as we may be that they violate a fundamental principle of God's created order of equality?

One remedy, of course, is to revise our ways of speaking, taking care to use inclusive language, to speak of "humankind" rather than "mankind," or of a "person" or "one" rather than the conventional pronoun "he." Inclusive language may be extended into the theological language of liturgy to speak of God as our

Heavenly Parent or as our Loving Father and Mother. One need not go to the extreme of "God/ess" or the "kingdom/queendom" of God, but care should be taken, especially in liturgy, to use inclusive language.

Much more crucial than the conversion of semantic habits, however, would be the changes in our social structures, in policies and practices of employment and promotion, to achieve a genuine equality of rights and privileges. As living costs rise, more and more wives have to work to help keep house and home together. When both husband and wife are employed and there are young children to be cared for, all sorts of troubles and problems arise. But a new and promising pattern of relationship is emerging, one that reflects a normative Christian ideal of vocation, in which husband and wife are equal partners who share the responsibilities of homemaking, and in which Dad can say, with no apology, "I'm a househusband," and Mom can say "I'm a housewife." By sharing equality at work and at home, they can manage. Not easy, but not impossible.

One final point: there is need still to overcome inequities between males and females through reforms in the laws of the land. Legal precedents still show chauvinistic preference for males over females in divorce and alimony matters, for instance, and in labor law. The proposed Equal Rights Amendment (ERA) has yet to gain formal support from a sufficient number of states to become national law. Many of the Religious Right oppose ERA because they claim it would undermine the American family. Yet, on balance, the case for ERA, as based on the Christian and democratic norms of equality and proportional justice, is stronger than the case against it.

9

Economic Ethics: Work and Vocation

We now move from the inner circle of intimate family ties and tensions and our relations with near neighbors of differing color or ethnic background to the larger circle of economics, from home and neighborhood to the office downtown, to the industrial plant, or wherever our workplace may be. In this chapter I address the question of the bearing that the Christian norm of *vocation*, or "calling," has on the *production* of goods and the ever-expanding "services and information" sectors of our economy. In the next chapter I turn the coin over and address the issues of the *consumption* of goods in our American economy and the moral issues involved therein.

As we enter the tangled moral maze of economic policies and practices, it may be well to recall the frame of double contextualism sketched in chapter 5. As outlined there, Christian decision is made at the interface between the faith and the facts. From the side of the faith-premises, I proposed that Christian ethical norms rest upon certain bottom-line theological faith-premises: the creating, sustaining, judging, redeeming actions of God. On this foundation rests the basic ethical norm of agape, the love of God and neighbor. Yet, as we confront the multiple and sometimes colliding claims of neighbors, we must translate the norm of love into policies of justice, which involve impartiality, equality, and an inequality proportional to differing needs and merits. On the other side, to make responsible and realistic choices, we must also confront the hard facts, the empirical circumstances that surround the choice. But these facts pose conflicting values that are built into the context, requiring difficult and sometimes painful preferences in which we must sacrifice one value to serve another. A Christian's conscience stands precisely at the nexus of choice between the moral "ought" of a loving justice and the "is" of the factual context, where all sorts of values collide.

How might this model be used as a way of doing ethics when we come to economics? At first sight, it looks like a long way indeed between the Christian faith-premises underlying the command of neighbor-love and such problems as the rights and wrongs of protectionism in international trade or the terms of a labor contract or the deregulation of the airlines. The Bible has nothing to say about protective tariffs or tax shelters or IRAs. The distance is so great that our conventional wisdom splits the realm of ethics of any kind, Christian or not, from the realm of economics. Economics in practice seems to be guided by its own rules. Though it is indeed a long way from Sunday's sermon on the parable of the Prodigal Son to the decision the bank officer must make on Monday morning about foreclosing a mortgage, all economic policies and practices have unavoidable ethical dimensions. What is now called the postindustrial age refers to much more than the assembly line at the plant; it refers also to the vast systems of services, information, management, banking and investment, both national and international.

The vast changes in the technologies of production, communication, and transportation have carried us far from the family farm that raised corn to sell in town. We now operate in a global economy, where the production of goods in America must compete with foreign imports made at a much lower wage scale, where the value of the dollar drops, and where the American trade deficit continues to mount. In this global economy, the questions about tariffs and protectionist legislation or about federal subsidies for farmers are more than can be answered by the simple cost-benefit equation of the economist. These issues, too, have ethical dimensions: the well-being of all members of the human family, those abroad and at home.

The Concept of Vocation in History

We might best start with the biblical norm of vocation and work. From the very start, according to the stories in Genesis, work had a religious meaning. Adam and Eve were charged by their Creator to "till and to keep" the garden of Eden. Throughout the Old Testament, the terms of God's covenant required faithful obedience to God's commands as the condition of his providential prospering of Israel. Three of the Ten Commandments—those prohibiting stealing, deceit, and coveting—have direct economic meaning. One chapter of the apocryphal book of Ecclesiasticus sets forth the religious ideal of all types of common work—carpentry, farming, sheepherding, blacksmithing. They "keep stable the fabric of the world, and their prayer is in the practice of their trade" (Ecclus. 38:34).

In biblical times, of course, work was done in a simple, primitive, rural culture, with the crudest of tools, close to the soil or to water, where everyone worked to maintain a bare subsistence. All were close to the edge of famine and starvation. Soil and streams were worked for the service of neighbor out of reverent obedience to the Creator and Sustainer of all life. Because "the earth is the LORD's and the fullness thereof," human beings were to be stewards, not owners of the land. Work in this primitive economy was a form of praise and prayer:

> Let the favor of the Lord our God be upon us,
> and establish thou the work of our hands upon us,
> yea, the work of our hands establish thou it (Ps. 90:16).

When the Hebrews entered into Canaan, the Jubilee Year celebration periodically freed all slaves and returned properties to their former proprietors or heirs, because the goods of God's earth were to be shared in common. Indeed, for the prophets of the Old Testament, authentic worship consisted not in ceremonial rites but in economic practices of care for the needy, the widow, the orphan, and the oppressed.

I can only sketch briefly the complex historical development of the concept of vocation from the early church to the present. As the Christian church grew in the Roman world and became established, there developed a two-story image of work, as an expression of the relationship of the church to the world. On the upper floor of the house of faith were the monks, nuns, and priests, who were practicing a "higher calling," living by the "counsels of perfection" in their ascetic practices of poverty, chastity, and obedience. Christians on the first floor were the "seculars," who engaged in the work of the world: housekeeping, farming, carpentry, whatever. As St. Francis described the ideal of his monastic order: "God has called us into this holy religion for the salvation of the world and has made this compact between the world and us, that we should give it good example and that it should provide for our necessities."[1]

With the Reformation, Martin Luther came to challenge this two-story scheme. His doctrines of justification by grace through faith alone and the priesthood of all believers mean that all persons, in whatever line of work, are equally called to serve their neighbors in love, out of glad response to God's forgiving grace in Christ. The work of a shepherd, a tradesman, a housewife—even that of a soldier—is as sacred as the work of the priest. Luther's commentary on the Christmas story expresses dramatically his concept of vocation:

> "And the shepherds returned, glorifying and praising God
> . . . ."
> This is wrong. We should correct this passage to read, "They went and shaved their heads, fasted, told their rosaries, and put on cowls." Instead, we read, "The shepherds returned." . . . and did exactly the same work as before. They did not despise their

service, but took it up . . . with all fidelity and I tell you no bishop
on earth ever had so fine a crook as those shepherds.[2]

John Calvin continued this Reformation theme in his reading
of the concept of vocation. Under God's benign but exacting
sovereignty, each Christian is assigned a "station," or calling,
where he or she fulfills the needs of the neighbor. Calvin's concept
of divinely appointed stations, like Luther's doctrine, puts all
persons on a common level, in a system of mutual interdependence. All work is dignified. The menial becomes holy. "No task
will be so sordid and base, provided you obey your calling in it,
that it will not shine and be reckoned very precious in God's
sight."[3] All persons are held accountable for integrity in their work,
under the eye of the Divine Lord of the universe.

From this doctrine of vocation, as framed by the great Reformers, developed what came to be known as the "Protestant work
ethic."[4] If the devout Protestant believed that work of whatever
sort was indeed a form of praise to God and service to neighbor, it
became a profoundly serious matter, with a distinctive syndrome
of values: diligence and care in work from dawn to dusk, frugality
and simplicity in lifestyle, because nothing should be wasted on
the sins of the flesh ("inner-worldly asceticism," as Max Weber
called it), thrift, and individual free enterprise. Also, by the terms
of the early capitalism developing in Western Europe, usury was
no longer prohibited: interest on capital was licit. The fruit of the
labor of the diligent Protestant farmer, merchant, craftsperson
followed inevitably: prosperity. An increased income became a
sign of God's favor. As the maxim put it, "God helps those who
help themselves." Poverty, once a virtue in the monastic orders,
became no longer a virtue. An echo of that value shift is heard in
the words of the traditional wedding ceremony: "For better, for
worse; for richer, for poorer."

In the preindustrial economy of the sixteenth and seventeenth
centuries, this Protestant work ethic was practiced in a rural or
small town setting, where the worker knew the neighbor for
whom the corn was being ground, the plow made, or the cowshed
built. This context of work in a small community enhanced a sense

of accountability, both to neighbor and God, for care and crafts-manship. The law of charity still guided economic activity. John Wesley, in his famous sermon "The Uses of Money," summarized the Protestant work ethic in three phrases: "Gain all you can, save all you can [by which he meant frugality], and give all you can." The eighteenth-century moral philosopher and economist Adam Smith defended free-enterprise capitalism with the assurance that the pursuit of prosperity by one person did not mean that another would thereby be deprived. For by simple multiplication, if I seek my well-being and you seek your well-being and another person seeks his or her well-being, we are all seeking the common good, as assured by the "Unseen Hand" behind it all.

The Secularization of Vocation

The industrial and organizational revolutions of recent centuries brought about a vast conversion in the concept of vocation, both in the internal motivations for work and in the outer conditions of work.

As Weber and Tawney and other economic theorists traced the story, the worker has experienced a subtle but profound change in the spirit that he or she brings to the daily tasks of life. The Calvinistic-Puritan concept of vocation as praise of God and service of neighbor changed to the Yankee work ethic. Benjamin Franklin epitomized this in many of the maxims of *Poor Richard's Almanac*:

> Early to bed, and early to rise,
> Makes a man healthy, wealthy, and wise.
>
> Then plow deep, while sluggards sleep,
> And you shall have corn to sell and to keep.

Free-enterprise capitalism under competitive conditions came to bless acquisitive instincts in all lines of work, so that one might rise in social class. The Calvinistic principle of faithful work in one's station shifted to a concern for economic "status." The Christian concern for neighbor still remains, yes, but it is no longer a sacrificial *caritas*. It becomes "charity," what one may give to the needy from what is left over when one has taken care of the needs and comforts of one's own household.

The gradual secularization of vocation, I might add, has had positive benefits. From the constraints of Calvin's doctrine of vocation as a fixed station, the new mobility of the economy opened up vocational choices. The shoemaker's son need not follow in his father's footsteps but could choose another line of work.

An even more profound impact on human work and the ideal of vocation took place in the *external* change in work brought about by the industrial revolution. The machine replaced the human hand in the production of goods. The ethical impact of the mechanization of common work has resulted in a mixed bag of goods and ills, blessings and curses.

On the benefit side, surely the machine has been a blessing in all the ways it has emancipated us from the weight of drudgery, the dull and menial tasks of Edwin Markham's "Man with the Hoe":

> Bowed by the weight of centuries he leans
> Upon his hoe and gazes on the ground,
> The emptiness of ages in his face
> And on his back the burden of the world.

The machine has freed human labor from drudgery in the field, in the kitchen, in building roads and homes, and myriad other workplaces. Obviously, too, the machine has increased enormously the productivity and efficiency in communication, in health care, in mining, in transportation, in business transactions, in education.

Anyone who has romantic notions about a pretechnological culture should reflect on how he or she might manage the household chores for one gray winter day without electric light or stove, or communicate a family emergency without a telephone.

But the story also has a negative side. In the automobile industry, a robot can perform an operation more efficiently and cheaply than a person. This increases the threat and the rate of unemployment in some basic industries, or at least requires the upgrading of jobs from assembly-line production to forms of employment for which skills of mind are needed. But "high technology and the service economy cannot begin to fill the void left when manufacturing jobs travel to the third world."⁵ This shift from labor-intensive to capital-intensive industrial production constitutes a darkening prospect in some urban centers of America. Look at the story of Bethlehem Steel in Johnstown, Pennsylvania, for example, where a number of factors conspired to bring that giant industry to the brink of collapse: the antiquated machinery reducing the efficiency of production, the tense battles between the labor unions and management, from which the contracts finally negotiated proved no-wins for both sides, and the competition from cheaper steel products imported from abroad.

Another negative impact of the industrial revolution and the mechanization of work are the various forms of alienation that seem to be their inevitable consequence. One form is the separation of the worker from what is produced. Whereas a craftsperson of the preindustrial age exercised at least a degree of personal skill, imagination, even creativity, in the handwoven fabric or the Chippendale desk, such personal involvement is now cut off by the machine. On the assembly line, in the textile factory, the employee performs one tiny function. She or he is a "hand," not a person.

Along with the industrial revolution has come what is known as the organizational revolution, the development of giantism in major industries. Although its rhetoric, ringing with the self-confidence of an Iacocca, is still that of early capitalism, "individual free enterprise," people in fact work within huge corporations. The small entrepreneur is an endangered species. Big farms swallow up the small farms, and big corporations absorb smaller firms. Despite the counterrevolution of recent decades, which have seen the recovery of many small independent economic enterprises, a new kind of cottage industry, the general trend is still moving toward giantism.

The consequence of all these revolutions is alienation of another sort in many kinds of work, a split between what one works *at* and what one works *for*, or between the work of the hand

and the motives of the heart. What I work *at* is the word processor, the derrick, or the bulldozer. What I work *for* are higher wages, longer vacation breaks, fringe benefits. To be sure, this alienation of hand from heart is not present in many kinds of common work, where the association with coworkers is close and morale is high, where one finds satisfaction of heart in a job well done. Nonetheless, many job operations are purely mechanical and might as well be done by a robot.

As the industrial revolution created the cities, a final form of alienation followed inevitably: the separation of homeplace from workplace. As recently as a century and a quarter ago, more than 90% of Americans lived and worked on their home farms; now approximately 4% of Americans are farmers. People "go to work" from home, usually into town or city. It's a common saying, "Oh, I don't live here—I just work here." And in the cities, even at the office, people do not know each other as they might in the neighborhood. We have impersonal, functional contacts, but the sense of community, of trusted intimacy (despite the jolly Christmas office party), is difficult to realize. We are transient strangers. Even people who live in the cities where they work often live in apartments. The word itself connotes separateness.

The Recovery of Vocation

In the face of these negative forces that seem to render the Protestant doctrine of vocation obsolete, how is it possible to recover the sense of meaningful vocation? If a foolish pastor should appear on the floor of an industrial plant in Detroit and shout *"Laborare est orare"* ("To labor is to pray") or "Work is the praise of God!" those who might hear these words above the clatter of machinery would be more likely to respond with profanity than with reverent approval.

It would be romantic folly to attempt to recover the sense of vocation by reverting to some preindustrial lifestyle, to go back to the farm, to escape to some Walden Pond, or to rid ourselves of all the machineries of our culture, as the Luddites tried to do in the midlands of England in the nineteenth century. No, the task is to find the strategies to humanize work within the giant systems of our technological economy and to combat as much as possible the forces of alienation I have described.

As noted, one of the essential elements in the original Protestant doctrine of vocation was a sense of meaning and purpose in the production of goods, a sense that went beyond the menial operation itself, so that what one worked at was linked to some human purpose—what one worked for. This sense created responsibility and accountability in work satisfaction. It is significant that many industries are using programs that represent, if only indirectly, an attempt to recover some moral meaning in work and to give workers a team sense and high morale. These practices—job rotation, job redesign, job training in new skills, for example—may not be inspired by a Christian intent, but their effect is certainly to humanize the work process. In some automobile manufacturing plants in Europe, such as Saab, and increasingly in this country, a team of mechanics assembles the products from beginning to completion rather than following the assembly-line procedure. Innovation in design suggested by workers is welcomed and tried out. This gives the team a sense of the whole and pride in the quality of the object. Many large high-tech industrial plants also offer recreational facilities, programs in aerobics, intramural sports, choral programs, arts and crafts programs, even individual psychiatric counseling. When such programs are adopted, the morale of the work force increases, for they express concern for the whole person, not just for the employee's function.

One of the most innovative economists who addressed the problem of recovery of vocation was E. F. Schumacher.[6] In books such as *Small Is Beautiful: Economics as if People Mattered*, and *Good Work*, Schumacher protested the axiom: bigger equals better. He called for the scaling down and decentralization of technology in ways that would be "gentle in its use of scarce resources and designed to serve the human person instead of making him the servant of machines."[7] He even grounded this case for small-scale technology in Buddhist teaching and the Beatitudes of the Sermon on the Mount. Although Schumacher's theories seem unduly romantic to many economists, his case for the decentralization of large industries and his concerns for persons over profits are being heeded in some quarters.

Still another way to recover a sense of vocation and meaning in work is through the rise of the labor union movement. Countering the established paternalistic power structures, in which the worker was only a hand in the textile mill, the labor movement gave the worker a voice and a vote in determining the conditions and policies under which she or he worked, in other words, a sense of personal worth. Although much conventional Protestant thinking remains suspicious of labor unions, remember that some of the inspiration for the growth of the labor unions came from the Protestant Social Gospel movement in the early decades of this century. This parallels the principles of Roman Catholic moral theology, which has long stood for the rights of labor to organize and bargain collectively. When a labor union is strong and democratically organized, when labor and management bargain "in good faith" to achieve fair wages and retirement benefits, and to provide grievance procedures, when each side makes concessions, even lowering its demands when the survival of the whole industry is at stake, a sense of community in the workplace is partially realized. Here the Christian meaning of proportional justice as defined in chapter 5 finds expression in economic practices.

One of the consequences of the labor union movement in America has been the rise in the wages of industrial workers. In our global economy this has meant that what is produced in Third World nations undercuts American products on the market, for the wage scale in those nations is much, much lower. This in turn creates a lowered market for American goods, forcing some industries such as General Motors to throw workers off the payroll. No simple ethical prescription can resolve this problem; the good of American workers seems to collide with that of workers abroad. To build high walls of protective tariffs and quotas on imports is to block free trade in the international economy. The most one can hope for is a "rough justice": through policies of free trade, the assistance from the International Monetary Fund, with aid to developing nations, the gap between the wealth of the developed nations and the stark poverty of the poor nations can be partially closed.

Yet the Christian sense of vocation and meaning in work cannot be recovered by these external systemic changes alone. They must be matched by an inner change in the heart with which one goes at one's work, whatever that may be. An essential part of such a will is to appreciate the interdependence of all work in keeping strong the fabric of community. Instead of "laddering" jobs on a scale of worth (executives high, manual laborers low), the normative concept of vocation would see all needful work on a par, in a democracy of service. The care and diligence of the welder on a spaceship or suspension bridge, the school-bus driver, the mail-sorter, the janitor, the bank teller, the elementary school teacher, are as crucial to community as is the work of the president of a firm.

The church, as the conscience of society, can and should make its prophetic witness to these problems in our economy. Through its worship, its educational programs, its preaching, and its policy positions, the church can bring to bear on these issues the norm of Christian vocation. It can breach the wall between ethics and economics and point to the ways vocation as meaningful work in the service of community can indeed be recovered. One of the most fruitful ways to do this would be to hold forums in which the ethical issues in many fields—medicine, law, business—might be addressed from a Christian perspective.[8] Thus might Sunday's worship be reconnected to weekday decisions and the meaning of God's calling to the service of neighbor at least partially restored.

10

Wasting and Wanting: The Ethics of Consumption

Now, to turn the economic coin over—from the supply side to the demand side, from the dynamics of production to the dynamics of consumption. The two are of course interconnected in a cause-effect relationship that runs both ways. The goods we consume determine the policies of production. At the same time, production profoundly influences what we consume.

The ethical issues of consumption can be approached by using again the double-contextualism frame of reference, wherein Christian ethical choice is made at the interface of the faith and the facts. The "oughts" are derived from the ideal norms of love and justice. Yet decision and choices must take realistic account of the circumstances that set limits on what is possible, which is always less than the ideal.

Consider first the empirical context, the prevailing patterns of our practices of consumption and the dynamics of consumerism. It takes little reflection to detect the values that guide most of our consumer choices: speed, power, comfort, luxury, efficiency, glamour, novelty—these seem to constitute the good life for the consumer. Consumerism decrees that we buy and use everything that promises these values.

To illustrate this claim, look at the values celebrated in the TV commercials that are fed into the homes of millions of Americans, whose TV sets are on five to six hours every day. Everything from automobiles to cheeseburgers and cold cereals is peddled by subliminal association with sexual glamour. Or, as you sit on an airplane, estimate the number of cans of Ginger Ale, Sprite, Coca-Cola, served on your flight. Multiply that by the number being served on every flight going across the country on that day. Where are all these empty cans dumped? Or if you should look out of the window of your 747 coming into O'Hare Airport in the evening, you would see below you the miles and miles of electric lights in metropolitan Chicago. How many quads of energy are needed to light the city? Or consider the waste of paper. One full Sunday *New York Times* issue of six hundred pages, laid end-to-end in a two-foot-wide row, would make a path seven hundred fifty feet long. A month's issues of the Sunday *Times* would make a path more than a half-mile long. Multiply that by the number printed and distributed. How many acres of forests in Canada or the West must be cut to provide the woodpulp to publish this number of papers? Or drive out to a shopping mall and you will find a K-Mart or a TOYS "Я" US occupying what looks like two acres of space, jammed to the ceilings with row on row of gadgets and devices that are being peddled as necessary to the bliss of your children. What would a Dorothy Day or a Mother Teresa think if she walked through such a jungle of goods? Or consider the fact that the number of motor vehicles in America is increasing twice as fast as the human population. Or consider the field of architecture. Until recently, architects designed homes and public buildings on the assumption of an inexhaustible supply of energy to heat and cool them. Only recently have energy-efficient principles begun to change architectural design so that renewable sources of energy are being used. Yet most new buildings are energy-wasteful. Or take a look at the scene of arrival on campus, around Labor Day, of the families bringing freshmen to enroll in colleges and universities. The station wagon is jammed full, perhaps towing a U-Haul trailer laden with all the clothes, the stereo, the word processor, the TV and the VCR, the ice cooler—all deemed bare necessities in the survival kit for a liberal education. Contrast that sight with the recollection that in the early nineteenth century young Thomas Carlyle walked the eighty miles from his home in Scotland to enroll at the University of Edinburgh, carrying in a backpack all his worldly goods, along, no doubt, with a Bible.

These snapshots are but glimpses of what seems to be the established American way of life. We are daily indoctrinated in the gospel of wealth and high consumerism. Salvation, not by the grace of God, but by gadgetry. The yuppie ethic and lifestyle seem to have displaced any remnants of the Puritan ethos.

The dynamics of this consumerism is defended by some economists on the grounds that the only way to keep an American economy healthy and its people employed is by producing more and more goods. The GNP must increase; otherwise, we are headed for a depression and disaster. And the way to make the graph line rise is to rid the American conscience of the last vestige of the Puritan principle that honored frugality and simplicity, to persuade consumers that what our forebears regarded as luxuries for the few are now necessities for the many. Moreover, material goods are manufactured to wear out faster, since built-in obsolescence is a guarantee of rapid turnover in the marketplace.

The barrage of TV advertising assaults not only the middle and the upper classes but the poor and the unemployed, who live in shabby tenements or shacks and who cannot possibly afford these fancy commodities. They, too, live in the constant sight of the mirage: the Nirvana of the young bronzed couple romping on a Florida beach or enjoying an elegant meal in a fancy hotel, thanks to "Master Card." "Buy now, pay later." (No mention is made of the hidden cost of credit payments.)

To be sure, not all advertising is deceptive and gross. AT&T offers its long-distance services with vignettes of families (usually minorities) exchanging affectionate greetings and "brought together," though geographically far apart. But by and large, the terms of the "good life" offered in ads of the daily paper or on TV are far from the "life abundant" promised by Christ.

This pattern of "galloping consumption" requires, of course, the increasing use of energy resources. In our capital-intensive economy, energy to fuel this consumption increases at a rate of 4% to 6% annually. According to many studies of our energy consumption, America loses about two-thirds of the energy it consumes, half from the inefficiency of machines and half from entropy waste.[1]

If we could move from our nests of cozy luxury and look at our accepted pattern of consumption from a global perspective, we would see startling evidence that should be weighed in the nexus of decision and choice. One is the disparity between American wealth and the dire poverty of many other parts of the world, especially the Third World. We who constitute 6% of the world's population consume more than 30% of the world's energy. The average American uses fifty times the amount of energy used by a person in India. While I am luxuriating in my hot shower, a child in the sub-Saharan region of Africa is walking three miles from her family's hut to a well, to draw the two buckets of water that will have to do for the cooking and washing for her whole family for the night. Or think of the family in Haiti who have no food at all for the day or the tiny medical clinic in rural Zaire that is attempting to provide minimal health care for some eight thousand people.

The Energy Crisis

We should also look at this phenomenon of high consumerism in a temporal frame, that is, the tension between the now and the future that arises from the high rate of consumption that in turn requires such high energy use. The many facets of the energy crisis are much too complex to be more than sketched here.[2] But, in brief, what is happening is that our high rates of production and consumption are exhausting the resources of the earth. We are mortgaging the future at a rate that future generations cannot possibly afford to pay. The fossil fuels, currently our main source of energy, despite apparent periodic oil gluts, are being exhausted, will become more and more expensive to extract, and will be gone soon after the year 2000. The alternative source, coal, destroys the environment. If coal is strip-mined, it causes soil erosion and ecological disaster. Depth mining has dire consequences for human health. The pollution from plants fueled by coal creates a greenhouse effect, warming the atmosphere, melting ice caps at the poles and raising sea levels along the coastlines. Acid rain pollutes the forests and lakes of the Northeast. In the 1960s and 1970s a safe and sure alternative source of energy came into use, one that seemed to resolve our problems: nuclear power. But in the 1980s this alternative has proved a chimera. With the risky incident at Three Mile Island, and the Chernobyl accident in the Soviet Union, confidence in nuclear power as the solution to our energy crisis has been shaken. Even with the safety measures taken in the building of plants, the costs now seem to outweigh the benefits. Many nuclear plants are being shut down, and plans for new ones are being cancelled. And where will the lethal radioactive waste from the existing plants be stored? Every state in the Union acknowledges that it has to be stored somewhere, but the citizens of every state protest that it should not be stored in their backyard.

Withal, we American consumers remain oblivious to the energy crisis and the moral costs of our high living. In 1979 President Carter issued a sharp warning in a prophetic speech. "In a nation that was proud of hard work, strong families, close-knit communities, and our faith in God, too many of us now worship self-indulgence and consumption. Human identity is no longer defined by what one does but by what one owns." Yet, he argued, "the events of the past decade have demonstrated that owning things and consuming things do not satisfy our longing for meaning."[3] In the years since, how many Americans have heeded the wisdom of Carter's words?

A Christian Ethical Response

In the face of these tangled dilemmas in our American patterns of consumption and the energy crisis, it is obvious that no quick-fix formulas or panaceas offer a clear way back from the precipice of disaster. Yet, just as obviously, unless there be some turnabout, some conversion in our lifestyle, the prospects for posterity are ominous indeed: an ecological genocide.

From the Christian faith and its ethical commands, we may derive inspiration and trust that if we return to the exacting terms of the covenant theology, we may recover a lifestyle in which we count on the One "who redeemeth thy life from destruction." God's judgment upon our sins of waste and our exploitation of nature is severe indeed, but God's forgiving grace is also ever-present. The basic theological premise for responsible consumption and ecojustice is that our God as creator provides the resources of the earth to meet human need, but only if we consume and use these resources responsibly. As the ethical norm for the production of goods discussed in the preceding chapter is *vocation*, the ethical norm for the consumption of goods is the norm of *stewardship*. John Calvin put it thus: "All the blessings we enjoy are Divine deposits, committed to our trust on this condition, that they should be dispensed for the benefit of our neighbors." This same norm in Christian ethical theory has held constant to the present. The theme of the 1979 Conference of the World Council of Churches (WCC), "Faith, Science, and the Future," was a "just, participatory and sustainable society."

The norm of responsible stewardship in consumption can be lived in several ways. One is to cut through the mirage of advertising and to learn to distinguish between real needs and artificial wants. There is wisdom in the prayer of one of the proverbs:

> Give me neither poverty nor riches:
>   feed me with the food that is needful for me,
> lest I be full, and deny thee,
>   and say, "Who is the LORD?"
> or lest I be poor, and steal,
>   and profane the name of my God." (Prov. 30:8–9)

This need not mean an ascetic austerity, but it would mean the adoption of a simpler lifestyle than the one into which we are daily lured by consumerism.

In the glut of things that surround us, the norm of a "simple"

lifestyle has a negative ring. It seems to connote a barren emptiness. Yet it need not be so. Simpler living enables us to escape from
the cage of things and to discover delights of the spirit and all that
truly enriches life. As Thoreau put it, "Most of the luxuries, and
many of the so-called comforts of life, are not only not indis-
pensable, but positive hindrances to the elevation of mankind."[4]
Thoreau's word from Walden Pond echoes the word of Christ: "a
man's life does not consist in the abundance of his possessions"
(Luke 12:15). The "life abundant" that Christ came to bring is one
that is "rich toward God." The ethics of responsible consumption
will buy and use what is needed for the health of body and the
enrichment of mind and soul.

It would be ridiculous to draw up here a laundry list of do's
and don'ts, consumer goods that the simple life of a true Christian
permits or those it prohibits. The Bible is not of any help as a
consumer's guide in the supermarket. But there are resources that
parents can teach their children or a group of committed adults in a
church group might use to learn how to practice responsible,
simpler consumption.[5] Consumer cooperatives and consumer
unions are organized ways of involving buyers in responsible
consumption. Consumer's guides, which, for example, provide
data about generic medicines (many of which are the same quality
but much less expensive than brand-name medicines), are of great
value, especially for those on limited incomes.

Yet another problem in the ethics of consumption arises from
certain factors in the technological and industrial revolutions.
Advances in medical science have extended the average lifespan of
an American citizen by approximately thirty-five years, from forty
a century ago to seventy-five now. More and more people live
longer and longer. At the same time industrialization has increased
exponentially the time off from work, for those who are employed
as well as those who are retired. As people retire earlier and live
longer, a grave ethical problem arises: how are we to fill our leisure
time? Another spin-off from the technological revolution is the
plethora of machines that play *for* us, reducing our capacity, with
all this leisure time on our hands, to learn to play ourselves, to

exercise creativity and imagination. As one wise commentator on American culture put it, "Technology has mastered the art of saving time but not the art of spending it."[6]

What we need to enliven leisure time and enrich the simple life is to learn how to play. Rather than watching and listening to people perform on TV, we might learn to play ourselves—guitar, piano, flute. Compare the mental agility and genuine enrichment in playing chess and the vacuity in turning the knobs of the video game. Drama, music, handcrafts, athletics—all offer ways of redeeming the longer spans of leisure from the emptiness and the disease of "spectatoritis."

A church can be a redemptive force in our secular culture. In its liturgy, the church can provide rich resources to answer the plea "Teach us how to pray." In its programs of sports and music and arts, with adults as well as youth, it can also meet the need "Teach us how to play."

In sum, against the prevalent American mirage that quality of life is in direct ratio to the quantity of possessions and gadgets one has, the corrective Christian ethical norm is that the truly rich life consists in glad service to the needs of neighbors and in the creative use of leisure time, which is authentic recreation.

Ecojustice in the Global Village

"We must learn to live more simply, that others may simply live." This compelling word from a recent WCC conference points to another positive way in which Christians may respond to the ecological crisis, which is one consequence of consumerism. Many economists and agronomists claim that the problems of poverty and famine in the poor nations of the world derive not so much from dwindling natural resources as from the maldistribution of food and other basic goods. While America wastes, Third World nations want. Here we confront a most complex problem. When Paul Ehrlich's *Population Bomb* and other demographic studies alerted us to the perils ahead in the population explosion—that the earth's population, 3 billion in 1960, will reach 7.2 billion by the year 2000 unless stringent measures are taken to control it—the alarm was sounded but not heeded. The dwindling resources of the earth cannot possibly sustain such an exponential population growth. Some analysts, such as Garrett Hardin, have protested that the appeals of American charities to obey the religious injunction to "feed the hungry" by sending food to the starving in Africa will simply postpone the ultimate disaster. An immediate generosity will prove a long-range cruelty. His "life-boat" ethic claims that for the current population of the world to take aboard those in the water clamoring for help would ultimately overload the whole boat and it would sink. So we should let the poor drown.

There is a more responsible answer than the life-boat ethic. It is obedient to the biblical prophetic command that we should "feed the hungry and clothe the naked." It would pursue policies that would share American wealth not only by sending food to those who are starving but, more important, by providing the agricultural technologies that would enable the poor nations to become self-sufficient, to develop their own systems of irrigation, reforestation, and farming. The work of the Church World Service, Bread for the World, CARE, Oxfam—all are direct expressions of the Christian ecological conscience. Government programs such as the Peace Corps and AID (Agency for International Development), which provide economic assistance to these nations, are expressions of the same social conscience.

Incidentally, electronic communications have proved a potential blessing. In earlier times, "our town" was small, and our vision of our neighborhood was narrow. Now we are made aware of those in the global village whom we never saw before, for the sight of the drought-ridden neighbors in Africa is vividly brought into our living room by satellite. Our consciences should be aroused by the sight.

But the poor and hungry are not only in Zaire and Haiti. They are also across town in South Boston, Brooklyn, Detroit, and in the country slums of Appalachia. These folk, too, need help. Again, distributive justice can help to close the gap. One example is a program of recycling paper, glass, aluminum, so that it is not wasted. Another is to recycle clothing, furniture, household goods, through such agencies as the Goodwill Industries or the Salvation Army. Still another is the Habitat for Humanity movement, in which professional carpenters and amateur volunteer helpers construct or rebuild and insulate decent housing in the slums of the inner cities of America and abroad.[7]

Ecojustice and Energy Resources

Finally, the issue of the sources of energy. If the threatening facts concerning oil, coal, and nuclear energy are accurate, what shall we do to maintain even our present level of production? Ever since the 1974 Club of Rome report alerted the scientific community to the "limits to growth," the evidence has mounted daily that we must shift the source of our power from oil, coal, and nuclear fission to renewable sources of energy. Solar and wind power are the best sources. The technology for developing those sources and for storing the energy of the sun to produce photovoltaic cells for electric lighting, for instance, are rapidly being developed. Energy-efficient homes are angled to make the best use of the sun's light. The salvific power of solar and hydro energy has limits, to be sure, especially in powering motor vehicles, but by the turn of the century, it would be technically possible for solar energy to produce 20% of the energy we need. This, along with the other conservationist measures outlined, may relieve, though it will by no means dispel, our ecological crisis.[8]

Lest the garden entrusted to our stewardship by the Creator be turned into a wasteland, all persons of conscience are obliged to conserve the earth. To conserve by the private, immediate decisions made daily in the supermarket or at the gas station but also by legislation to protect wilderness areas from commercial developers, to enforce the Clean Air Act, to hold industries to the standards of pollution control, to provide state and federal funding for the development of renewable energy sources. Through such measures, the garden we are entrusted to "till and to keep" may provide for our lives now and for generations to come.

11

Christian Ethics and Politics

We come finally to the outside circles in the application of Christian ethical norms to our common life: politics. In this chapter I measure American political policies and practices by the standard of Christian love translated into justice.

Any analysis of Christian ethics and politics requires that we first remove a block that is deeply embedded in our "conventional wisdom," the prevailing hold of the familiar metaphor "the wall of separation" between church and state. This phrase, incidentally, appears nowhere in the Constitution or the Bill of Rights. But under the spell of this metaphor, people commonly interpret the relationship of church and state to mean the complete separation of Christian faith and ethics from politics. The Christian life has to do with inner spirituality, prayer, faith, salvation in Christ, devotion, as expressed in private acts of fidelity and kindness. Politics is the secular realm of power relations, wheeling and dealing, as expressed in the administration of government. Though politicians may use the rhetoric of religion in their speechmaking, the real name of their game is power play.

Yet a more careful look at the American political heritage reveals that the wall of separation is a misleading metaphor. It does not describe what historically has been and in many ways still is the normative understanding of the relationship of Christian faith to American democracy.

In 1796 President George Washington said, "And let us with caution indulge the supposition that morality can be maintained without religion. . . . Reason and experience both forbid us to expect that National morality can prevail in exclusion of religious principle." Thomas Jefferson, in his first inaugural address, spoke of America as "enlightened by a benign religion . . . acknowledging and adoring an overruling Providence, which by all its dispensations prove that it delights in the happiness of man here and his greater happiness hereafter." In 1984 the same conviction was voiced by President Reagan: "The truth is, politics and religion are inseparable. And as morality's foundation is religion, religion and politics are necessarily related."[1]

"Congress shall make no law respecting an establishment of religion, or prohibiting the free exercise thereof." This, the first clause of the Bill of Rights, applying at the outset to the federal government and only later, with the passage of the Fourteenth Amendment, to the separate states, is the legal form in which this ideal found expression. It bespeaks the ideal of a "benevolent neutrality"; i.e., the government should honor the vital place of religion in public life by allowing it free exercise. That is the state's benevolence. At the same time, in the face of religious pluralism, the state may not give a favored status to any one church. That is its neutrality, expressed in the establishment clause.

A complete separation of church and state is impossible. Religious belief and its consequent social expression involve relations with the state and its laws, sometimes conformity and sometimes collision. Ever since the 1878 Superior Court ruling against the Mormon practice of polygamy as counter to the common moral standard of monogamy, we have acknowledged the legitimate restrictions that the state, through law, may impose on religious institutions. Ever since the abolitionist movement, sparked by the

Christian conscience for human rights and against the institution of slavery, we have seen again and again the attempts of church bodies to influence legislation and politics that express their religious convictions. On legislation protecting the rights of minorities, the economic rights of labor, on budget policies dealing with poverty and hunger here and abroad, as well as on nuclear armaments and world peace, the churches and synagogues of America have importuned the state with the prophetic witness of the Old Testament prophets and of Christ, calling for justice and mercy as the true expression of the worship of God. The question then becomes, not whether religion and politics should mix, but what form that inevitable mix should take, in ways that do proximate justice both to the establishment clause and the free exercise clause of the First Amendment.

At the other end of the spectrum from the separationist norm is the Christian crusading ideal, a position that has come on strong in recent decades, championed by the Religious Right. Conservative evangelical groups such as Jerry Falwell's Moral Majority movement, now rebaptized the "Freedom Federation," Pat Robertson, and other like-minded televangelists have called for a crusade for a Christian America.[2] In the face of the deterioration of the moral fabric of American life, the alarming rise of the crime rate, the mounting rate of divorce and teenage pregnancies, signaling the erosion of American family values, the pervasive dangerous trends in public education to teach "secular humanism," they evangelize for a return to the Christian values that have made America great, a bastion of Christian virtue, strong and secure against godless communism.

The particular values the Religious Right celebrates are the pietistic values of a pure and holy life in keeping with what it takes to be biblical precepts. These include individual free-enterprise capitalism rather than socialistic economies, and the recovery of traditional family values by prohibiting pornography, homosexuality, abortion, and sex education in the schools. America should recover its true soul by reintroducing prayer and Bible study in our public schools, by electing only Christians to public office, and by building a strong military defense against the threat of communism, for as Falwell claims, "Nowhere in the Bible is there a rebuke

for the bearing of armaments."³ The mix of religion and politics
that the Religious Right and other conservative Protestants pro-
pose is clear: pietistic morality should be made public policy. The
church should be in politics up to its steeples.

Christian Ethical Premises of Democracy

In contrast both to the champions of complete separation and
those who would restore America to its Christian foundations by
enacting into law what they consider essential biblical principles,
the approach here is "Christian realism." It has historic roots in the
prophetic strands of the Bible and in the theology of Augustine,
John Calvin, and the proponents of the Social Gospel. Its most
influential modern spokesperson has been Reinhold Niebuhr.⁴ The
greater part of Niebuhr's professional career was spent wrestling
with the problems of politics in relationship to Christian ethical
norms. In this struggle he found the separatist position unrealistic
and irresponsible. Were he alive today, no doubt he would find the
Religious Right a fanatic form of idolatry.

The basic thesis of Christian realism as to the relationship of
Christian ethics to political systems and practices is that the ethical
norms of Christian community—love and justice—provide the
inner moral vitality, the *elan vitale*, to the outer structures of
American democratic systems and practices. To speak of the inner
moral vitality is to speak of the will, the habits of the heart, of
persons living within a democratic society.

To spell out this normative position of Christian realism, we
first acknowledge that the state or the political order is a given in
the order of God's creation. This given is not exactly in the Pauline
sense that "the powers that be are ordained of God" (Rom. 13) but
the sense that in any system of societal relationships there is
always some implicit or explicit locus of authority, some rules
guiding the traffic of social interaction, all the way from the simple
order of a family circle or a school or a PTA or a university to the
more formal and explicit terms of the town council, the state and
federal governments, and the United Nations. To be a person in a
society is always to be in some kind of political order. There is no
such thing as a nonpolitical existence.

But if the *fact* of the state is a given in God's created order, the *form* of the political order varies widely along a spectrum between the systems in which power is centralized and those in which power is distributed. A basic element of the democratic *credo* is the doctrine of popular sovereignty: "Governments derive their just powers from the consent of the governed." This doctrine is based on a trust that the common good is more likely to result when sovereignty is extended to the many rather than held by the few, as in totalitarian forms of government. Yet realism acknowledges that neither the federal nor the state government can function as a giant town meeting, where everyone has a chance to make a speech. That would be anarchy. Thus, in our American system of constitutional democracy, the elected officers, legislators and executives, representing their constituencies, have delegated powers.

What Christian moral premise justifies this system? *Vox populi, vox dei*? Is the quantity of opinion inevitably connected to the quality of opinion, so that one is assured of the moral good of the society on any issue by counting more noses? Not necessarily. The majority may be wrong. We should recall that the founders of our American government feared "mobocracy" as much as they protested the tyranny of the British crown. Only "enlightened" public opinion, they affirmed, can be safely entrusted with the franchise. Here, the Christian ethical norms of love and justice become relevant to democratic politics. When the will of the people is a benevolent will, that is, a will to elect officials and support policies that serve the higher good of the greater number rather than the narrower good of special interests, democracy becomes a healthy community. And what gives impetus to such a benevolent will? Christian love translated into the norm of justice. This is the first Christian moral premise of constitutional democracy, captured in the famous aphorism of Reinhold Niebuhr: "Man's capacity for justice makes democracy possible."[5]

Democracy as a Dike Against Sin

A second premise of the relationship of Christian ethics to democratic political theory stands in a dialectical relationship to the first. It is aptly put in the second part of Niebuhr's statement: "Man's inclination to injustice makes democracy necessary."

This premise is the view of human nature that is especially

strong in the Protestant tradition: the doctrine of human sin. Countering the benevolent will is the continual perversion of that will by the sin of hubris, pride, the arrogance of power, whereby people seek not the common good but their own privilege, power, and prestige, using the political system to lord it over others. Because human beings are political sinners, the systems of government must check and restrain that sin. As John Calvin put the matter: "The vice or imperfection of men therefore renders it safer and more tolerable for the government to be in the hands of many, that they may afford each other mutual assistance and admonition, and that if anyone arrogates to himself more than is right, the many may act as censors and masters to restrain his ambition."[6]

The influence of this Calvinistic principle was strong among the framers of the American Constitution, especially James Madison, who greatly feared "factions." This premise is the moral logic for the system of checks and balances and for the separation of powers between the legislative, judicial, and executive branches of government, each of which is a constitutional check against the others. For example, the Chief Executive may veto an act of Congress, but the countercheck empowers the Congress to override a veto by a two-thirds majority vote. The President may nominate persons to serve as Justices on the Supreme Court, but only with the "advice and consent" of the Senate.

This structure of government is much less efficient than the swift decrees of totalitarian dictatorship, but the moral reason for its worth is that the good of the whole is protected from the tyranny of any one of the parts. It requires an inner spirit of sufficient contrition to acknowledge one's own bias and prejudice. So the human "inclination to injustice makes democracy" as the separation of powers "necessary."

"To Secure These Rights"

The third distinctive feature of the democratic *credo* has to do with human rights. Jefferson's Declaration of Independence affirmed that "life, liberty, and the pursuit of happiness" are God-given rights that the state should secure. The Bill of Rights ensures state protection for the exercise of freedom of worship, freedom of speech, freedom of the press, freedom of assembly, and many others.

Significantly, the first clause of the Bill of Rights has to do with freedom of religion. In the long history of Western political thought this issue was battled in the religious wars that followed the Reformation. In nations where one or another church was the official religion, there were horrendous persecutions and slaughters of heretics. In America, before the Revolution, the Puritan colonies of Massachusetts and the Anglican colonies of Virginia denied religious rights to dissidents. In the seventeenth century, four Quakers were hanged on the Boston Commons for their heretical beliefs.

The battle for freedom of conscience and the other rights was fought on religious grounds. Sectarians such as Roger Williams, a Baptist, and William Penn, a Quaker, who claimed their right of religious belief and worship, did so out of an obligation to a power higher than the state. The biblical phrase "We must obey God rather than man" is the theonomous ground for claiming the rights of conscience against the political prescription of a certain mode of worship, belief, and action that might follow from that belief.

This historical point, that rights claimed against the state's power are grounded in obligation and responsibility that transcend the state, gives us a clue to a normative moral position for exercising rights in ways that maintain the health of democracy and protect it from deteriorating into anarchy. Rights and freedoms must always be linked with obligation and responsibility; otherwise, the exercise of rights tears the fabric of community.

Take freedom of speech and press, for example. Correlated to the exercise of that right is the obligation to speak or print the truth. Obviously, there are always divergent views about the truth of any matter addressed or reported. Yet, unless journalists exercise that right responsibly, they are rightly subject to laws against libel and slander. As a famous Supreme Court decision affirmed, the right to free speech does not allow one to cry "Fire!" in a crowded theater when no such threat exists. Even so, prosecution of the violation of basic freedoms through the judicial system can touch only the outer and most blatant distortions of truth. In the common daily exercise of free speech, the intercourse of democratic community relies upon a kind of honor system. It requires an ethics of civility and accountability that is willed from within by those involved in social intercourse.

Or take the rights of conscience in freedom of worship. The obligation correlate to this right is the will to allow others to worship in ways different from one's own, or not to worship at all, unless such worship and the ethical practices following from it endanger common health and safety, as in the Jonestown cult or in snake-handling rites.

In Article One, "the right of the people peaceably to assemble, and to petition the Government for a redress of grievances," what is the obligation correlate to this right to protest? Plainly, the protest is to be made peaceably, not violently, and presumably, if the grievance is redressed, the obligation is to dis-assemble.

Finally, civil rights, such as the right to vote or the rights of employment or equal educational opportunity. Normatively speaking, I may lay claim to these rights for my particular race, class, gender, religion, nationality, only if I acknowledge those rights across the board for those of different color, class, sex. As discussed in chapter 6, the Christian will to justice that obliges one to seek equal rights for all is the propelling force of conscience that underlies this universal extension of rights. If we are inclined to take this for granted, it is sobering to reflect that not until 1920, with the ratification of the Nineteenth Amendment, were women allowed to vote in national elections. And the Equal Rights Amendment is not yet ratified.

These basic human rights are protected by the system of law in the courts. More significantly, they are "secured" in a democratic society by its citizens' inner will to honor the sacred worth of all persons. There are secular, humanitarian premises for this will, but for a Christian, the ground for this spirit is theonomous: to honor the sacred worth of all persons as creatures of God, to whom we are ultimately accountable.

In sum, democratic policy has three Christian premises or foundations which protect it from tyranny or anarchy: the benevolent will, which validates popular sovereignty; the recognition of human sin, which requires the separation of powers; and the ethical obligation and responsibility that underlie the claims for human rights and freedoms.

Christian Ethics and Legal Justice

The validity of these norms may be tested and applied in many areas of common life in American democratic culture. Perhaps the most crucial concerns our system of law enforcement. The relationships of ethics to law and jurisprudence are complex and tangled. I can only sketch some of the main issues.[7]

Several theories prevail about the relationship of law to ethics. The "natural law" theory, derived from the Roman Catholic scholastic tradition, holds that there are certain divinely set norms and laws, discernible by human reason, by which the validity of specific laws can be measured. Though broad and general, they are immutable. Natural law covers many principles: that good is to be sought and evil avoided, the principle of private property for common use, the sanction of the monogamous family unit, the right of a family to nurture children in the true faith, the universal right to education and employment, the doctrine of the "just war," by which a nation may defend itself by force of arms. It is the task of the courts not to *create* laws but to *apply* these principles of natural law to particular cases so that justice may be done.

A second theory of law, commonly called positivism, is quite the opposite. By this view, there are no fixed, immutable moral norms set by the hand of God in the universe. As Justice Frankfurter once said, "The one rule of law is that there are no absolutes." Rather, laws are the expression of power interests, prevailing custom, "a prophecy of what the courts will decree." This positivistic theory of law is generally prevalent in legal education. In the courts, the justice done depends on whether the lawyer for the prosecution or the lawyer for the accused argues the more convincing legal precedent to the jury.

A third view of law comes from the evangelical Protestant tradition, which takes the Bible as its Supreme Court and reads the Bible as an inerrant and infallible norm for all human laws. For example, Holy Scripture justifies the support of free-enterprise capitalism, since, according to Jerry Falwell, "The free-enterprise system is clearly outlined in the Book of Proverbs."[8] The prohibitions against homosexuality, divorce, and women's rights are justified on biblical grounds. Some years ago, the former Secretary of the Interior, James Watt, a devout Bible-believing Christian, testified before a congressional committee that he need not pursue policies that protected the environment for posterity because the book of Revelation prophesied the imminent close of the age, so there would be no posterity for whom the environment should be protected.

Each of these theories of law has obvious shortcomings. The natural law theory, framed in the agrarian medieval age, cannot take into account the cultural and technological changes that may render some of its norms obsolete. Does the norm of "private property for common use" provide clear guidelines for legal decisions regarding corporate industries today? And the doctrine of the just war may be rendered obsolete by atomic weaponry (more on this in the next chapter).

The positivistic view of law, although realistic in its pragmatism and its sensitivity to plural and transient cultural circumstances, veers dangerously close to anomie and anarchy. The laws of the land and the decrees of the court become an expression of power interests and shrewd legalese rather than an application of the norms of justice to particular circumstances.

Likewise, a strict biblical fundamentalism, taking all the ethical mandates of the Bible as equally binding, will hardly suffice. Many biblical mandates contradict each other. Slavery is approved in the Old Testament, even in the Decalogue, yet the Christ of the New Testament calls for liberation of the oppressed. One divine command of the Old Testament is for the Israelites to "slaughter the Amalekites"; an injunction of the New Testament is to "love our enemies." Christ's words "I came not to bring peace but a sword" run counter to his mission "to guide our feet into the ways of peace." Biblical literalism is hardly a reliable foundation for modern jurisprudence.

A more realistic and responsible normative position would

acknowledge the truth in these three positions but would also attempt to overcome their fallacies. A Protestant approach to law and criminal justice would affirm that legal proceedings of the courts are indeed more than power plays. Ethical issues lie close underneath particular positive laws. The legal system of the state has the obligation to seek justice through due process in court proceedings. Such practices as trial by jury, court-appointed lawyers for the accused, presumption of innocence—all have an ethical ground, inherited from English common law. It is the obligation of the state, in dealing with crime, to steer a careful course of justice that on the one side ensures the safety and protection of society against crime and on the other punishes the offender, yet in a manner that is fair and proportionate to the seriousness of the offense.

The courts and the police powers of the state are constantly confronted with colliding claims and rights that must be adjudicated. In such matters as divorce proceedings; in the vexing question of abortion, in which the woman's right to choose is pitched against the fetus's right to life; in conflicts between private property and public interest, in which the economic interests of commercial developers run smack against the protection of land and water resources; in the right of privacy, which may conflict with the public's right to know through a free press—these and countless others are part of the daily grind of the law-making and law-enforcing machinery. No simplistic formula of "love thy neighbor as thyself" can solve them. The most that one can expect is a rough justice that will proximate the highest possible common good.

Penal Justice

A problem that should be of urgent concern for the Christian community today is that of criminal justice and penology.[9] No one needs to be reminded of the mounting rate of violent crime in America. Though more visible, albeit no less serious than white-collar crime, street crimes of murder, arson, larceny, rape, burglary, and the destruction of property are rampant. Just take a look at the morning paper. Whatever the causes, be they economic forces that widen the gap between rich and poor or the celebration of violence on TV or the ready availability of deadly weapons, a responsible society must cope with this alarming trend. To deal with this, our penal system attempts to do proximate justice to the collision of values between the security and safety of a society on the one hand and regard for the rights of the offender on the other. Proximate justice is the goal of the process of arrest, trial, and, when the offender is found guilty, sentencing in fair proportion to the seriousness of the offense. The usual sentence, of course, is time in prison.

Unfortunately, here we meet another grievous problem: the barbarism of life in most American prisons. To take but one example, North Carolina, which has one of the lowest crime rates in the United States, has one of the higher ratios of its population serving time in prison. Some eighteen thousand prisoners are housed in prisons built to accommodate fourteen thousand at the most, and a majority of them are there for nonassaultive crimes. Thousands more are in jail awaiting trial, presumed innocent unless proven guilty. Many awaiting trial are there because they are too poor to post bail. Of the persons sentenced to prison, only approximately 20% were sentenced for crimes of violence (murder, kidnapping, sexual assault, manslaughter, robbery), and more than two thousand of these prisoners are under twenty-one years of age.

The living conditions in the prisons are horrendous. Violence, sexual harassment, drug use, racial tension and brawls, stealing, and the brutality of prison guards turn prisons into "schools of crime." It is this harsh fact, that inmates are schooled in sharpening their criminal skills, that accounts in part for the high rate of recidivism, i.e., the return of offenders to serve prison terms.

What should be a normative Christian response to this dark situation? One certainly would be that of preventive medicine, that is, for society to legislate social welfare measures to alter the economic conditions that give rise to crime, so that fewer people would be driven to stealing, fleecing, mugging, or drug abuse. Another response would be "community service" sentences, which are rendered at the discretion of the judge and which in many cases prove to restore the offender to responsible behavior.

Another redemptive step is a monitored parole practice. According to penologists, the rate of recidivism is markedly lower when a monitored parole system is practiced. Still another is separate court proceedings for juvenile delinquents and adult offenders.

Finally, a Christian moral obligation is to improve the conditions within the prison walls for those serving sentences for serious crimes. If the criminal justice system is rightly to call itself the Department of Correction, rehabilitation programs of job training, education and recreational activities, more liberal visitation privileges, and chaplaincy services to provide counseling and worship are concrete expressions of the Christian ethical norm of justice tempered with mercy. Christian justice is more than retributive. It also seeks to redeem the offender to responsible citizenship. Such movements as OAR (Offender Aid Restoration) and the Yokefellow Prison Ministry are supportive organizations of church persons who seek to practice the forgiving word of Christ's love for those in prison.

Finally, what about the morality of capital punishment? Although the Supreme Court ruled in 1972 against capital punishment on the constitutional ground that it was "cruel and unusual punishment," the Court more recently has reversed itself and upheld some lower court decisions permitting the death penalty for certain heinous crimes. The question has evoked sharp divergence and heated debate in the Christian community. The case for capital punishment as voiced by the Religious Right is made partly on the biblical grounds of *lex talionis*, "retaliation" ("Whoever sheds the blood of man, by man shall his blood be shed," Gen. 9:6), and partly on the pragmatic grounds that capital punishment deters serious crime.

The case against capital punishment, as affirmed by the mainline Protestant churches in their various social policy statements, is more convincing. For one thing, there is no evidence that taking the life of a criminal convicted of first-degree murder does indeed act as a deterrent against others who might commit such crimes. The crime rate is no lower in the states or nations that have enforced the death penalty than in those that have not. More important, the Christian case against the death penalty is based on the ethical premise that justice should be loving, in response to the theological premise of divine redemption, which goes beyond divine judgment. The final purpose of punishment and law enforcement is not revenge, or simply retribution, but restoration and rehabilitation.

The proponent of capital punishment might protest that imprisonment for life, under the conditions in our prisons, is worse than death, a kind of living hell. The answer to this argument is not, however, to legitimize the death penalty but to improve the conditions of our prisons and to extend the boundaries of the parole system so that the criminal may be restored to a more responsible and law-abiding way of life.

12

International Relations and the Nuclear Crisis

At first glance, the issues of foreign policy might seem the furthest from our day-to-day concerns. Worries about a strained romance or marriage or completing all academic requirements by the end of the semester or coping with a minor ailment in one's car or one's body are much more pressing than the threat of a nuclear war or the issue of military aid to the contras in Nicaragua or terrorism in the Mideast. Yes, we read the headlines and know that these are troubled times, but the troubles are way over there, far from our personal existences.

Yet a closer look would make us realize that these issues hit close to home. Foreign affairs become domestic affairs that cannot be avoided. They affect the mundane decisions of my daily life, my heart, and my conscience, as well as my family budget. When we citizens file our income tax forms, we know—or should know—that approximately 40% of our taxes go to the Department of Defense. If I am a parent whose children are heading for college, I learn with dismay that federally funded loans for their education may be drastically cut in order to maintain America's lead or parity in the arms race. Workers in a textile plant find their jobs threatened by federal policies of international trade, over which they have no control. Or a member of the board of trustees of a university is confronted with a choice about divesting funds in the corporations that do business with South Africa. Or what about a nuclear physicist who is working on research for the Strategic Defense Initiative (SDI, or "Star Wars") at the Lawrence Livermore Laboratory and who is becoming more and more convinced of the technical folly as well as the destructive peril of the total enterprise? Caught in such dilemmas as these, what should one do, as guided by a Christian conscience?

As a matter of fact, the issues of foreign policy affect our daily lives closely, and the mushroom cloud casts a dark shadow over all our affairs. We should not have been surprised to learn that in 1985 students at Brown University were supplied with suicide pills that could be used in the event of a nuclear holocaust. According to a recent study, a majority of high school students fear the threat of nuclear war so strongly that they do not expect to live their normal life span.[1]

Let us set these problems again within the framework of double contextualism, a frame that puts the moral nexus of conscientious decision at the interface of the facts and the faith, between the empirical realities of the current world scene and the high normative principles derived from Christian theology and ethics.

First, the facts. Luke 2:1 reads, "a decree went out from Caesar Augustus that all the world should be enrolled." At the time of Christ's birth, the connotation of the word *world* was a very limited, parochial one: a tiny segment of the Mediterranean, under the control of the Roman Empire. Now, the word *world* requires a global definition. Through extended travel and trade, plus scientific techniques in communication, we have become neighbors in a global village. By electronic communication, the neighbors on the other side of the globe are brought close on our TV screens. A satellite from America can read a license plate in Moscow. On the evening news we see a bloody riot in Soweto, two heads of state shaking hands at a summit meeting in Geneva, guerrilla forces in action in the jungles of Nicaragua, starving children with bloated stomachs in Zaire. Jet planes can carry us halfway around the world in half a day.

In this global village, a fact of paramount importance is that we are economically interdependent. No nation is an island unto itself, economically self-sufficient. The American economy relies on oil from the Middle East, coffee beans from Latin America, tea from the Orient, and pulpwood from Canadian forests. Russia purchases grain from America. America sells Coca-Cola to the Orient and buys cars and cameras from Japan.

But herein is the dangerous dilemma: though people in the global village are economically interdependent, each precinct in the village operates under a political system of independence, of national sovereignty. Each nation is a law unto itself, determining its policies to protect its national interests and territorial rights. And America's national interests and security extend far beyond our geographic borders, to the Persian Gulf and Central America. Formed after World War II, the United Nations comes closest to an expression of world government, but no one of the major powers that make up the Security Council feels accountable to that world government or the International Court of Justice when its ruling collides with national self-interest.

A third ominous fact of the international situation is the East-West polarization of power, between the nations of communist ideology that make up the Warsaw Pact and the nations of democratic heritage that make up NATO. Within these two clusters, of course, the United States and the USSR are the dominant superpowers.

A fourth hard reality is the imbalance of power and wealth between the United States and the Third World. To put the contrast in stark terms: if one conceives the population of the world as 1,000 persons, 60 of that number would be citizens of the United States, and 940 would be citizens of other nations. The 60 Americans enjoy half the income of the world; the 940 must share the other half.

A fifth factor has to do with population growth and ecology, to which I referred in chapters 9 and 10. The high consumerism of the industrial nations of the West can be carried only at an increasing cost to the world's natural resources. At the same time, the population explosion continues, especially in the poorer nations, despite stringent measures such as those the Peoples Republic of China imposes to limit family size. How can the earth sustain this imbalance? Economic and ecological issues become entangled with political ones.

Finally, the most crucial fact of all is the changed character of weaponry. Starting in 1945 with the development of the atomic bomb, the technical sophistication and the proliferation of nuclear weapons have grown at an exponential rate. More than fifty thousand nuclear warheads are now stored or deployed worldwide, most of them in the United States and the Soviet Union, the use of any one of which would cause incalculable destruction. All international dealings go on under the dark threat to human life itself and a nuclear winter for the whole environment.

Values in Conflict

The collision of values in this complex of facts is a tangled one. For one thing, the economic interdependence of the peoples in our global village has made us rely on each other for goods and services. Yet the political principle of national sovereignty leads to alienation and hostility. For another, the values of peace (*shalom*) often collide with the values of justice. This was at the heart of the debate in the 1930s, before World War II. Hitler's gross violation of human rights in the imprisonment and slaughter of six million Jews as well as his invasions of Czechoslovakia and Poland proved an injustice so great that the Allied Nations were finally compelled to sacrifice the values of peace to make war against the Nazi regime. Though we speak easily of a "just and lasting peace," there are many times in foreign affairs when these two values do indeed collide. When the USSR invades Afghanistan, when it denies basic human rights to dissidents within Russia, imprisoning them or exiling them to Siberia, should the response of Western nations be "Peace be with you" or "Let justice be done"? In South Africa, where a small white minority denies basic political rights to blacks under the system of apartheid, should Americans be pacific or should they demand justice through stringent economic sanctions that would compel change in the structure of South Africa's government?

Finally, values collide in all the conflicts between the USSR and the United States that are brought about by the development of nuclear weapons. The bottom-line collision is not between the value of a free society and the value of a totalitarian society; the collision is between the life and health of the whole of humanity on the one hand and the destruction of human life on the other, leaving the cockroaches to inherit the earth.

Normative Christian Response to the Sovereignty of God

To recall the basic terms of the covenant theology, outlined in earlier chapters, faithful, ethical Christian action is a response to the creative, judging, and redeeming activity of God, the Lord of all life and history. Response to God the creator is the defense and protection of the given order of *shalom*, in obedience to the One who has created all peoples "to dwell on the face of the earth together."

The authentic response to God's judgment is to acknowledge that we constantly break that peace through the sin of pride and national arrogance and therefore in contrition and humility to acknowledge that America is not God.

The sin of self-righteousness is an ailment endemic to the foreign policies of all nations. When the President of the United States speaks of the Soviet Union as an "evil empire," the implication of that snide remark is that America is a virtuous empire, a bastion of pure civility. This pride leads an American family sitting around the dinner table to say "Well, we just don't trust the Russians." They would not expect a family in Leningrad, sitting around their dinner table, to say "Well, we just don't trust the Americans." To be sure, heads of state do not come to summit meetings and open their sessions by chanting *Kyrie eleison* ("Lord, have mercy"). But the authentic response to God's judgment should be contrition. Actually, has the record of American policy, both foreign and domestic, reflected benevolent virtue? In contrition we should recall our past and present treatment of Native Americans, our confinement of the Japanese-Americans in internment camps on the West Coast during World War II, our invasion of Grenada, or the government's disinformation (a euphemism for lying) to deceive the Libyan government. The deceptions and cover-ups of the federal administration in the Iran-contra affair that came to light late in 1986 could hardly be called models of integrity. And which nation among the superpowers was the first and only nation to use atomic weapons in time of war? The bomb dropped on Hiroshima killed or maimed 130,000 civilians; at Nagasaki a few days later, 75,000. Thousands more died later from the aftereffects of the blast. The benign excuse of President Truman that this act would shorten the war and save lives did not cover this crime against humanity. All these acts hardly qualify America to claim innocence before the throne of God's judgment. Although we may rightly protest the violation of human rights in other nations, we, too, have violated human rights. We, too, have blood on our hands.

Yet because the Christian faith also relies on a God who forgives and redeems, whose grace follows his judgment, the third form of response to that grace is to become peacemakers, to seek all the ways to restore the *shalom* broken by national pride and to become channels of grace in the global village. It is this trust in the ever-present divine grace that prompts gracious living, not only in our private lives but in our foreign policy as well, that we may become—to use the prayer of St. Francis—"instruments of your peace."

Christian Ethical Norms in History

Three classic positions describe how Christians should respond to collision and strife among nations.[2] The first is pacifism, which includes several forms. One is vocational pacifism, the position espoused by sectarian groups such as the Quakers or Mennonites, who refuse to participate in war in any form, whatever the national policy. The second form of pacifism calls upon the nation to become peacemaker. In this view, pacifism would not be just the witness of an individual or a sect against the state but would become foreign policy itself. It was this type of pacifism that ran strong in the 1920s and 1930s in the democratic nations of the West. A third form of pacifism, which has appeared since the development of nuclear weaponry, might be called nuclear pacifism, that is, the support for national defense measures that might maintain conventional weapons, but a denial of any use of nuclear weaponry on the moral grounds that no justice could follow from resorting to weapons of mass destruction.

In complete opposition to these versions of pacifism is the "holy war" position. When Christianity became the official religion of the Roman Empire under Constantine, the cause of Christ came to be identified with the cause of the Roman state. The cross was emblazoned on the shields of the Roman soldiers. During the Crusades, Christians were called to do battle against the infidels, the Turks, so that Christendom and the Holy Roman Empire might be extended.

Not just a quaint artifact of ancient history, this crusading ideal appears anew in the rhetoric of the evangelists of the Religious Right. They champion America as the last fortress of freedom, "the land of the free and the home of the brave." They call on Christians to protect and extend this freedom by increasing armaments and to do battle if necessary against the great enemy, "the godless Communism of the USSR." The warrant for this holy war stance, according to Jerry Falwell, is a biblical one. "Nowhere in the Bible is there a rebuke for the bearing of armaments." Therefore, "It is now time . . . to increase American military preparedness."[3]

In between pacifism and the holy war position is a third stance, the "just war" policy. It is an attempt to balance realistically the competing values of *shalom* and international justice. Derived from the Catholic scholastic tradition of the Middle Ages, it affirms that under certain licit circumstances one nation may resort to war, but only in accord with certain moral principles: that the cause be just, that the final intent be to restore peace, that war be taken as a last—not a first—resort, that war be declared by proper governmental authority, and that there be a reasonable prospect of success. While a war is being waged, two further principles are to be observed: first, that it be fought in a just manner, using weapons that discriminate between military and civilian objectives, and protecting the rights of prisoners of war. Second and similar is the principle of proportionality: that the damage inflicted should be proportionate to the moral ends sought.[4]

What Shall We Do to Survive?

A Christmas card received in December 1945 was dated: Year 1 A.B. This was its message: "Not a star in the East, but a pillar of fire has ushered in our new world. Humanity now more urgently than ever before must choose to live in the spirit which the star heralded, or to die beneath the fire."

The buildup of nuclear arsenals (weapons now with destructive power 1,600,000 times the power of the bombs dropped on Hiroshima and Nagasaki) requires a "substantially new manner of thinking," as Albert Einstein said, for a normative answer to the ways the human race may survive on this planet. Even more than the religious communities, the scientific community, particularly physicists such as the Union of Concerned Scientists both in America and in the Soviet Union, has raised the cries of alarm about the perils of nuclear war. The scientists' fears have been supported by the policy statements of ecumenical church bodies and denominational boards.[5]

Their common message is this: nuclear weaponry has made the doctrine of the just war obsolete. A nuclear war cannot be waged justly, distinguishing military and civilian objectives or observing the norm of proportionality. No system of civilian defense can protect the citizens of urban centers from the immediate or long-range effects of a nuclear exchange. This is the testimony of the International Physicians for Prevention of Nuclear War, some 150,000 from forty-five different countries, including the USSR. A "limited nuclear war" is an impossibility. Moreover, the high technology of nuclear weaponry has rendered obsolete the distinction between defensive and offensive weapons.

Consider this staggering fact: according to a Department of Defense report, "a single multi-kiloton nuclear weapon detonated

125 miles over Omaha, Nebraska, could generate an electro-magnetic pulse strong enough to damage electric currents throughout the entire US and Canada and Mexico and bring their economies to a halt."

The Pros and Cons of Deterrence

One policy position strongly supported by the Republican administration is that of maintaining a parity of power in equivalent nuclear arsenals. On the correct premise that the technology of nuclear weaponry is here to stay, the only way to keep the peace is by the fear of "mutual assured destruction" (MAD). The threat of nuclear retaliation will deter the other side from a first strike. As Caspar Weinberger has said, "Deterrence provides security by convincing potential adversaries that the risks and costs of aggressions will exceed any conceivable gain." On the occasion of the commissioning of the *Michigan*, a Trident submarine carrying nuclear warheads, the Director of the Naval Propulsion Program said, "The *Michigan* and its crew must be so good at something that none of us want to do, that we shall never have to do it." So, the only way to keep the peace in the nuclear age is by maintaining the balance of terror.

Although Pope Paul VI conceded the moral validity of deterrence as an "interim ethic," but only as a step toward progressive disarmament, the United Methodist Council of Bishops' Pastoral Letter calls the policy of mutual deterrence "idolatry." The fallacy in deterrence is that it does not bring the security it promises, for each side in the arms race has to keep several megaton steps ahead of the other. Given the dynamics of nuclear scientific development, an absolute parity of power is impossible. Further, as the Pastoral Letter points out, the policy of deterrence puts an unwarranted trust "in the rationality of decision makers," in which there is no assurance against nuclear holocaust.[6]

The SDI, proposed by President Reagan as a purely defensive measure against possible nuclear attack, is flawed, technically and morally. Even if it were to prove 99% effective against incoming nuclear warheads (which many nuclear physicists doubt), the 1% that penetrated the shield would wipe out most American cities.

And with the line between offensive and defensive now blurred, one cannot call SDI an entirely defensive measure. This fact has prompted "3,700 science and engineering professors, including fifteen Nobel laureates and 57% of the faculties at the nation's top twenty physics departments, to sign a petition pledging to refuse SDI funding."[7] In a recent poll, 80% of the members of the National Academy of Science opposed SDI.

Another ethical issue in the SDI proposal is its cost, which James Schlesinger estimated at one trillion dollars. Add that to the cost of maintaining our arsenal of nuclear and conventional weapons, and the moral issue of economic justice becomes overwhelmingly evident. "The 1988 Defense Authorization bill reported by the House Armed Services Committee calls for spending $288 billion, or $9,132.40 per second."[8] Funds for health, education, and welfare, both at home and abroad, must be slashed to carry this load.

Christian Witness for Peace

It follows from all this analysis that persons of conscience must become peacemakers, in whatever way we can. Whatever may be done at the summit meetings of heads of state, much must also be done in the plains and valleys, among concerned peace-making citizens, so that our voices may be heard at the summit.

The phrase "in defense of Creation" might sound odd, especially to a person working in the Department of Defense. What the phrase refers to, however, is not our national self-defense. Rather, it means that the whole order of God's creation—the ecosystem and all of humanity—has been placed in jeopardy by the development of atomic weaponry and is threatened with destruction. All persons of conscience should act to save God's created order.

The starting point is a conversion of the heart and will from fear, distrust, and the arrogance of power to a new trust in the grace of God which can sustain a commitment to peacemaking. Yet this change of heart must also issue in praxis and in social action.

Where to start? One measure would be, in the spirit of Christ, "to break down the dividing wall of hostility," to overcome the habit of "bloc" thinking, in which Russia is thought of as the Kremlin, the Politboro, the KGB, failing to see the citizens of the Soviet Union as persons who share with us common hopes and fears, indeed, as persons who suffered the loss of twenty million Russian lives in World War II and whose anxiety for peace has been deepened by that pathos. One way to overcome bloc thinking is through cultural exchanges among athletes, musicians, dancers, artists, scientists. Exchange programs of scholars between universities in the Soviet Union and the United States can help to change our stereotypes. Under the auspices of denominational bodies, visits by American Christians to the Soviet Union and the visits of Russian Orthodox churchpeople to America can overturn many of the suspicions and distrusts and build bridges of understanding. Major conferences of the World Council of Churches—in which the Eastern Orthodox Church, numbering fifty million members, is a leading denomination—recover the sense of unity among Christians, a sense that transcends political barriers. Making such connections is a vital form of peace education.

Christian churches in the valleys can be peacemakers by political action. When a local city council endorses a nuclear freeze policy, when a community such as Cambridge, Massachusetts, declares itself a nuclear-free zone, when physicists are led by conscience to withdraw from R&D projects of the defense industries, when interdenominational bodies lobby in Washington for arms reduction, these are actions—successful or not—that are faithful to the Gospel. Some actions go further, such as when Archbishop Hunthausen in Seattle encouraged the Roman Catholics in his diocese to withhold 50% of their income tax payments. "The war-tax resistance" movement is a radical expression of conscientious objection to American foreign policy.

But the most pressing imperative is progressive bilateral nuclear disarmament. Chairman Gorbachev's proposals for reductions in nuclear weapons should be met by comparable reductions on our part. A stumbling block that brought the Iceland summit to a temporary halt in the fall of 1986 was the Republican administration's refusal to back down on SDI research and deployment. But signals are being given that some progress in nuclear arms reduction can be made. The 1988 agreement on mutually verifiable reduction and the elimination of short- and medium-range nuclear missiles is a realistic step toward an accord of peace. It is a sign that both sides agree covertly that the real power conflict is not between the two superpowers but between nuclear weaponry and the future of the whole human race. The most urgent moral task for Christians is to witness in defense of God's created order that we citizens of the global village and our posterity can learn to live in peace.

Notes

1: The Challenge of Secular Culture to Christian Ethics

1. Harvey Cox, *The Secular City: Secularization and Urbanization in Theological Perspective*, rev. ed. (New York: Macmillan, 1966), p. 17.
2. One systematic defense of this "religion" is Michael Novak, *The Spirit of Democratic Capitalism* (New York: Simon & Schuster, 1982).
3. See Robert Bellah's essay "Civil Religion in America" (originally published in the winter 1967 issue of *Daedalus*), which can be found in Russell E. Richey and Donald G. Jones, eds., *American Civil Religion* (New York: Harper & Row, 1974). See also Bellah, *The Broken Covenant: American Civil Religion in the Time of Trial* (New York: Seabury Press, 1975). Bellah traces well the clear trend from Secularization I to Secularization III in the relationship of Christian faith and American democracy, in which America becomes a kind of god and patriotism the new piety.

2: The Field of Christian Ethics

1. Edward LeRoy Long, *A Survey of Christian Ethics* (New York: Oxford University Press, 1967), is a useful overview. For a compendium of major types in historical sequence, see Waldo Beach and H. Richard Niebuhr, eds., *Christian Ethics: Sources of the Living Tradition*, 2nd ed. (New York: Random House, 1973). Another source of historical materials is George W. Forell, ed., *Christian Social Teachings: A Reader* (Garden City, N.Y.: Anchor Books, 1966).
2. H. Richard Niebuhr, *The Responsible Self: An Essay in Christian Moral Philosophy* (New York: Harper & Row, 1963).
3. See James Gustafson, *Protestant and Roman Catholic Ethics: Prospects for Rapprochement* (Chicago: University of Chicago Press, 1978). See also Roger Mehl, *Catholic Ethics and Protestant Ethics*, trans. James H. Farley (Philadelphia: Westminster Press, 1971).
4. Ernst Troeltsch, *The Social Teachings of the Christian Churches*, trans. Olive Wyon, 2 vols. (New York: Macmillan, 1931); and H. Richard Niebuhr, *Christ and Culture* (New York: Harper, 1951).
5. Gustafson, *Protestant and Roman Catholic Ethics*, p. 94.
6. Beach and Niebuhr, *Christian Ethics*.
7. See, for example, Paul Abrecht, ed., *Faith and Science in an Unjust World*, vol. 2, *Reports and Recommendations* (Geneva: World Council of Churches, 1980).

8. See George F. Thomas, *Christian Ethics and Moral Philosophy* (New York: Scribner, 1955).

3: The Faith-Premises of Christian Ethics

1. The first parts of Karl Barth's *Church Dogmatics* are a thorough explication of Protestant theological faith. More recently, James M. Gustafson, *Ethics from a Theocentric Perspective*, vol. 1, *Theology and Ethics* (Chicago: University of Chicago Press, 1981); and J. Philip Wogaman, *A Christian Method of Moral Judgment* (Philadelphia: Westminster Press, 1976); are simpler treatments of these matters.
2. See Joseph L. Allen, *Love & Conflict: A Convenantal Model of Christian Ethics* (Nashville: Abingdon Press, 1984).
3. Karl Menninger, *Whatever Happened to Sin?* (New York: Hawthorn Books, 1973).
4. Reinhold Niebuhr, *The Nature and Destiny of Man: A Christian Interpretation*, vol. 1, *Human Nature* (New York: Scribner, 1941), chs. 7, 8, 9, represents the most influential explication of the Protestant conception of human sin in modern Christian ethical literature.

4: Christian Ethical Norms

1. See Anders Nygren, *Agape and Eros*, trans. Philip S. Watson (Philadelphia: Westminster Press, 1953); Gene H. Outka, *Agape: An Ethical Analysis* (New Haven: Yale University Press, 1972); and C. S. Lewis, *The Four Loves* (New York: Harcourt, Brace, 1960); for a detailed analysis of the different meanings of Christian love.
2. See Anders Nygren, *Agape and Eros*, trans. Philip S. Watson (Philadelphia: Westminster Press, 1953); Gene H. Outka, *Agape: An Ethical Analysis* (New Haven: Yale Univesity Press, 1972); and C. S. Lewis, *The Four Loves* (New York: Harcourt, Brace, 1960); for a detailed analysis of the different meanings of Christian love.

5: Christian Love and Social Justice

1. For a comparable treatment of this scheme of doing ethics, see Roger Lincoln Shinn, *Forced Options: Social Decisions for the 21st Century* (San Francisco: Harper & Row, 1982); and ch. 2 of Waldo Beach, *The Wheel and the Cross: A Christian Response to the Technological Revolution* (Atlanta: John Knox Press, 1979).
2. John A.T. Robinson, *Christian Morals Today* (Philadelphia: Westminster Press, 1964); and Joseph Fletcher, *Situation Ethics: The New Morality* (Philadelphia: Westminster Press, 1966), and *Moral Responsibility: Situation Ethics at Work* (Philadelphia: Westminster Press, 1967).
3. See Gene H. Outka et al., eds., *Norm and Context in Christian Ethics* (New York: Scribner, 1968); and John C. Bennett et al., *Storm over Ethics* (New York: United Church Press, 1967); for the varied reactions to "situation ethics."

4. Robert Frost, "To a Young Wretch," in *Collected Poems* (New York: Holt, Rinehart & Winston, 1964).
5. Fletcher, *Situation Ethics*, p. 87.
6. See José Míguez Bonino, *Doing Theology in a Revolutionary Situation* (Philadelphia: Fortress Press, 1975), and *Toward a Christian Political Ethics* (Philadelphia: Fortress Press, 1983); and Gustavo Gutiérrez, *A Theology of Liberation: History, Politics, and Salvation* (Maryknoll, N.Y.: Orbis Books, 1973).

6: Sexuality, Marriage, and Christian Love

1. See publications of the Alan Guttmacher Institute, in particular, *11 Million Teenagers: What Can Be Done about the Epidemic of Adolescent Pregnancies in the United States?* (New York: Alan Guttmacher Institute, 1976). A report by SIECUS (Sex Information and Education Council of the United States) claims that each year 40% of all sexually active girls aged fifteen to nineteen become pregnant.
2. *Newsweek on Campus*, April 1984, p. 21.
3. Kenneth Keniston and the Carnegie Council on Children, *All Our Children: The American Family under Pressure* (New York: Harcourt Brace Jovanovich, 1977).
4. *The Hymn Book of the Anglican Church of Canada and the United Church of Canada* (Toronto, 1971), no. 202.
5. For a parallel discussion of this issue from a psychologist's perspective, see Robert J. Trotter, "The Three Faces of Love," *Psychology Today*, September 1986, pp. 46–50, 54.
6. One example can be found in the statement on homosexuality in "Social Principles," in *The Book of Discipline of the United Methodist Church* (Nashville: United Methodist Publishing House, 1984), p. 90.
7. James B. Nelson, "Homosexuality and the Church," *Christianity and Crisis* 37 (April 4, 1977):66. Interestingly, this same liberal position is defended by several prominent American Roman Catholic theologians. See Anthony Kosnik et al., *Human Sexuality: New Directions in American Catholic Thought* (New York: Paulist Press, 1977).
8. *Newsweek*, August 10, 1987,
9. Yale Kamisar, "Drugs, AIDS and the Threat to Privacy," *New York Times Magazine*, September 13, 1987, pp. 109–14.

7: Birthing and Dying

1. See Paul Ehrlich, *The Population Bomb* (New York: Ballantine Books, 1968); and J. Philip Wogaman, ed., *The Population Crisis and Moral Responsibility* (Washington, D.C.: Public Affairs Press, 1973).
2. "Resolution on Responsible Parenthood," of the General Conference of the United Methodist Church (1976), reaffirmed in the statement "Social Principles" (1984), and published in *We Affirm* (Washington, D.C.: Religious Coalition for Abortion Rights, 1984), p. 6.

3. The Presbyterian Church, U.S., "The Nature and Value of Human Life" (a statement, publication 8984, adopted by the 121st General Assembly) (Atlanta: Presbyterian Church, U.S., 1981), p. 15.
4. "A Call to Concern" was published in *Christianity and Crisis* 37 (October 3, 1977), pp. 223-25.
5. Roe V. Wade, 93 Supreme Court 705 (1973). A useful discussion of this abortion problem is to be found in James B. Nelson and Jo Anne Smith Rohricht, *Human Medicine: Ethical Perspectives on Today's Medical Issues*, rev. ed. (Minneapolis: Augsburg, 1984).
6. See Nelson and Rohricht, *Human Medicine*, p. 87.
7. Matt Clark, "When Doctors Play God," *Newsweek*, August 31, 1981, pp. 48–54.

8: Racial and Gender Relations

1. One of the standard classical studies of this matter was written by the psychologist Gordon W. Allport, *The Nature of Prejudice*, abr. ed. (Garden City, N.Y.: Doubleday, 1958).
2. See Robert S. Lecky and H. Elliot Wright, eds., *Black Manifesto: Religion, Racism and Reparations* (New York: Sheed & Ward, 1969); Joseph C. Hough, *Black Power and White Protestants: A Christian Response to the New Negro Pluralism* (New York: Oxford University Press, 1968); and Charles V. Hamilton and Stokely Carmichael, *Black Power: The Politics of Liberation in America* (New York: Random House, 1967).
3. See Martin Luther King, Jr., *Strength to Love* (New York: Harper & Row, 1963), and *Where Do We Go from Here: Chaos or Community?* (New York: Harper & Row, 1967). See also Kenneth L. Smith and Ira G. Zepp, Jr., *Search for the Beloved Community: The Thinking of Martin Luther King, Jr.* (Valley Forge, Pa.: Judson Press, 1974).
4. James H. Cone, *A Black Theology of Liberation* (Philadelphia: Lippincott, 1970), and *For My People: Black Theology and the Black Church* (Maryknoll, N.Y.: Orbis Press, 1984).
5. In the large body of material now emerging on a religious perspective on the feminist movement, the following are a few of the best: Rosemary Radford Ruether, *Sexism and God-Talk: Toward a Feminist Theology* (Boston: Beacon Press, 1983), and *Womanguides: Readings toward a Feminist Theology* (Boston: Beacon Press, 1985); Mary Daly, *Pure Lust: Elemental Feminist Philosophy* (Boston: Beacon Press, 1984); and Carol P. Christ and Judith Plaskow, eds., *Womanspirit Rising: A Feminist Reader in Religion* (San Francisco: Harper & Row, 1979).

9: Economic Ethics: Work and Vocation

1. *The Little Flowers of St. Francis* (London: Burns Oates, 1953), p. 131.
2. Roland H. Bainton, ed. and trans., *The Martin Luther Christmas Book* (Philadelphia: Westminster Press, 1948), p. 50.

3. John Calvin, *Institutes of the Christian Religion* (Philadelphia: West-minster Press, 1960), bk. 3, ch. 10, par. 6.

4. R. H. Tawney, *Religion and the Rise of Capitalism* (London: J. Murray, 1926); and Max Weber, *The Protestant Ethic and the Spirit of Capitalism*, trans. Talcott Parsons (1920; reprint, New York: Scribner, 1958).

5. John C. Raines and Donna C. Day-Lower, *Modern Work and Human Meaning* (Philadelphia: Westminster Press, 1986), p. 40.

6. E. F. Schumacher, *Small Is Beautiful: Economics as if People Mattered* (New York: Harper & Row, 1973), and *Good Work* (New York: Harper & Row, 1979).

7. Schumacher, *Small Is Beautiful*, p. 154.

8. Dennis Campbell, *Doctors, Lawyers, Ministers: Christian Ethics in Professional Practice* (Nashville: Abingdon Press, 1982).

10: Wasting and Wanting: The Ethics of Consumption

1. See, for example, *National Geographic Magazine*, February 1981, an issue on energy, and Donella H. Meadows et al., *The Limits to Growth: A Report for the Club of Rome's Project on the Predicament of Mankind*, 2nd ed. (New York: Universe Books, 1974).

2. A good overview is Barry Commoner, *The Closing Circle: Nature, Man, and Technology* (New York: Knopf, 1972). See also *Newsweek*, July 16, 1979, for a special report on the energy crisis.

3. Quoted in an article by David Shi, "What Happened to the Simple Life," *National Humanities Newsletter*, Spring 1986, p. 2. See also Shi's *The Simple Life: Plain Living and High Thinking in American Culture* (New York: Oxford University Press, 1985).

4. Henry David Thoreau, *Walden and Other Writings*, ed. Brooks Atkinson (New York: Modern Library, 1937), p. 13.

5. Center for Science in the Public Interest, *99 Ways to a Simple Lifestyle* (Garden City, N.Y.: Anchor Press, 1977).

6. George Soule, *Time for Living* (New York: Viking Press, 1955), pp. 100–1; also quoted in Robert Lee, *Religion and Leisure in America* (New York: Abingdon Press, 1964), p. 260.

7. Millard Fuller, *No More Shacks! The Daring Vision of Habitat for Humanity* (Waco, Tex.: Word Books, 1986).

8. For further positive responses, see Dieter T. Hessel, ed., *Energy Ethics: A Christian Response* (New York: Friendship Press, 1979); and Roger Lincoln Shinn, *Forced Options: Social Decisions for the 21st Century* (San Francisco: Harper & Row, 1982).

11: Christian Ethics and Politics

1. A lively account of this matter, which often comes under the rubric "civil religion," is to be found in the writing of Robert Bellah; see his essay "Civil Religion in America," in Russell E. Richey and Donald G.

Jones, eds., *American Civil Religion* (New York: Harper & Row, 1974) (essay originally published in the winter 1967 issue of *Daedalus*), and *The Broken Covenant: American Civil Religion in Time of Trial* (New York: Seabury Press, 1975).

2. Jerry Falwell, *Listen, America!* (Garden City, N.Y.: Doubleday, 1980).
3. Ibid., p. 98.
4. See in particular Reinhold Niebuhr, *The Children of Light and the Children of Darkness* (New York: Scribner, 1944); Harry R. Davis and Robert C. Good, eds., *Reinhold Niebuhr on Politics: His Political Philosophy and Its Application to Our Age Expressed in His Writings* (New York: Scribner, 1960); and Ronald H. Stone, *Reinhold Niebuhr: Prophet to Politicians* (Nashville: Abingdon Press, 1971).
5. Niebuhr, *The Children of Light and the Children of Darkness*. For a more thorough treatment of this dialectical issue, see Waldo Beach, *Christian Community and American Society* (Philadelphia: Westminster Press, 1969), ch. 7.
6. John Calvin, *Institutes of the Christian Religion* (Philadelphia: Westminster Press, 1960), bk. 4, ch. 20, par. 8.
7. See Harold J. Berman, *The Interaction of Law and Religion* (Nashville: Abingdon Press, 1974). See also *The Journal of Law and Religion*, begun in 1983, sponsored by Hamline University School of Law and Council on Religion and Law.
8. Falwell, *Listen, America!* p. 13.
9. See L. Harold DeWolf, *Crime and Justice in America: A Paradox of Conscience* (New York: Harper & Row, 1975).

12: International Relations and the Nuclear Crisis

1. The United Methodist Council of Bishops, *In Defense of Creation: The Nuclear Crisis and a Just Peace* (Nashville: Graded Press, 1986), p. 60.
2. Roland H. Bainton, *Christian Attitudes toward War and Peace: A Historical Survey and Critical Re-evaluation* (Nashville: Abingdon, 1960), is a classic study of this issue.
3. Jerry Falwell, *Listen America!* (Garden City, N.Y.: Doubleday, 1980), pp. 98, 100.
4. See the Pastoral Letter of the National Conference of Catholic Bishops, *The Challenge of Peace: God's Promise and Our Response* (Washington, D.C.: United States Catholic Conference, 1983). See also the United Methodist Council of Bishops, *In Defense of Creation*, pp. 30–36.
5. See, for example, the policy pronouncements of the World Council of Churches from its 1979 conference "Faith, Science, and the Future," as found in Paul Abrecht, ed., *Faith and Science in an Unjust World*, vol. 2, *Reports and Recommendations* (Geneva: World Council of Churches, 1980); or comparable statements from the National Council of Churches and various mainline Protestant denominations. See also

Gordon D. Kaufman, *Theology for a Nuclear Age* (Philadelphia: Westminster Press, 1985).

6. United Methodist Council of Bishops, *In Defense of Creation*, p. 48. See also George Kennan, *The Nuclear Delusion: Soviet-American Relations in the Atomic Age*, rev. ed. (New York: Pantheon Press, 1983), and Jonathan Schell, *The Fate of the Earth* (New York: Knopf, 1982).

7. *Newsweek*, September 12, 1987, p. 88. See also the book based on studies conducted by the Union of Concerned Scientists, *The Fallacy of Star Wars*, ed. John Tirman (New York: Vintage Books, 1984).

8. *Common Cause*, September/October 1987, p. 10.

Further Reading

1: The Challenge of Secular Culture to Christian Ethics

Bellah, Robert, et al. *Habits of the Heart: Individualism and Commitment in American Life.* New York: Harper and Row, 1986.

Childress, James, and David Harned, eds. *Secularization and the Protestant Prospect.* Philadelphia: Westminster Press, 1970.

Clebsch, William. *From Sacred to Profane America: The Role of Religion in American History.* New York: Harper and Row, 1968.

Cox, Harvey. *The Secular City: Secularization and Urbanization in Theological Perspective.* Rev. ed. New York: Macmillan, 1966.

———. *Religion in the Secular City: Toward a Postmodern Theology.* New York: Simon and Schuster, 1984.

Ellul, Jacques. *The Technological Society.* Translated by John Wilkinson. New York: Knopf, 1964.

Meland, Bernard. *The Secularization of Modern Cultures.* New York: Oxford University Press, 1966.

Slusser, Gerald. *A Christian Look at Secular Society.* Philadelphia: Westminster Press, 1968.

Toffler, Alvin. *Future Shock.* New York: Random House, 1970.

———. *The Third Wave.* New York: Morrow, 1980.

2: The Field of Christian Ethics

Beach, Waldo, and H. Richard Niebuhr, eds. *Christian Ethics: Sources of the Living Tradition.* 2nd ed. New York: Random House, 1973.

Gustafson, James. *Christ and the Moral Life.* New York: Harper & Row, 1968.

———. *Protestant and Roman Catholic Ethics: Prospects for Rapprochement.* Chicago: University of Chicago Press, 1978.

Long, Edward LeRoy. *A Survey of Christian Ethics.* New York: Oxford University Press, 1967.

———. *A Survey of Recent Christian Ethics.* New York: Oxford University Press, 1982.

Niebuhr, H. Richard. *Christ and Culture.* New York: Harper, 1951.

White, R. E. O. *Christian Ethics: The Historical Development.* Atlanta: John Knox Press, 1981.

3: The Faith-Premises of Christian Ethics

Barth, Karl. *Church Dogmatics.* Vol 3, pt. 4. Translated by G. T. Thompson et al. New York: Scribner, 1936–.

_____. *The Knowledge and Service of God according to the Teachings of the Reformation.* Edited by John T. McNeill and translated by Ford Lewis Battles. New York: Scribner, 1939.

Calvin, John. *Institutes of the Christian Religion.* Bks. 1, 2. 2 vols. Philadelphia: Westminster Press, 1960.

Gardner, E. Clinton. *Biblical Faith and Social Ethics.* Pts. 1–4. New York: Harper, 1960.

Gustafson, James. *Theology and Christian Ethics.* Philadelphia: United Church Press, 1974.

_____. *Ethics from a Theocentric Perspective.* 2 vols. Chicago: University of Chicago Press, 1981–84.

Niebuhr, H. Richard. *Radical Monotheism and Western Culture.* New York: Harper, 1960.

Niebuhr, Reinhold. *The Nature and Destiny of Man: A Christian Interpretation.* 2 vols. New York: Scribner, 1941–43.

Tillich, Paul. *Love, Power, and Justice: Ontological Analyses and Ethical Applications.* New York: Oxford University Press, 1954.

_____. *The Dynamics of Faith.* New York: Harper, 1957.

Wogaman, J. Philip. *A Christian Method of Moral Judgment.* Philadelphia: Westminster Press, 1976.

4: Christian Ethical Norms

Allen, Joseph L. *Love & Conflict: A Covenantal Model of Christian Ethics.* Nashville: Abingdon Press, 1984.

Beach, Waldo. *The Christian Life.* Chs. 3–7. Richmond, Va.: CLC Press, 1966.

DeWolf, L. Harold. *Responsible Freedom: Guidelines to Christian Action.* New York: Harper & Row, 1971.

Niebuhr, H. Richard. *The Responsible Self.* New York: Harper & Row, 1963.

Outka, Gene H. *Agape: An Ethical Analysis.* New Haven: Yale University Press, 1972.

Williams, Daniel. *The Spirit and the Forms of Love.* New York: Harper & Row, 1968.

5: Christian Love and Social Justice

Bennett, John. *The Radical Imperative: From Theology to Social Ethics.* Chs. 1–5. Philadelphia: Westminster Press, 1975.

Brunner, Emil. *Justice and the Social Order.* New York: Harper, 1945.

Hauerwas, Stanley. *Vision and Virtue: Essays in Christian Ethical Reflection.* Notre Dame, Ind.: Fides Publishers, 1974.

Maguire, Daniel. *The Moral Choice.* Garden City, N.Y.: Doubleday, 1978.

Niebuhr, Reinhold. *Love and Justice: Selections from the Shorter Writings of Reinhold Niebuhr.* Edited by D. B. Robertson. Philadelphia: Westminster Press, 1957.

Outka, Gene H., et al., eds. *Norm and Context in Christian Ethics*. New York: Scribner, 1968.

Smedes, Lewis. *Choices: Making Right Decisions in a Complex World*. San Francisco: Harper & Row, 1986.

Thomas, George F. *Christian Ethics and Moral Philosophy*. Ch. 11. New York: Scribner, 1955.

Tillich, Paul. *Love, Power, and Justice: Ontological Analyses and Ethical Applications*. New York: Oxford University Press, 1954.

6: Sexuality, Marriage, and Christian Love

Fairchild, Roy. *Christians in Families: An Inquiry into the Nature and Mission of the Christian Home*. Atlanta: John Knox Press, 1964.

Greeley, Andrew, ed. *The Family in Crisis or in Transition: A Sociological and Theological Perspective*. New York: Seabury Press, 1979.

Hettlinger, Richard. *Sex Isn't That Simple: The New Sexuality on Campus*. New York: Seabury Press, 1974.

Jersild, Paul, and Dale Johnson, eds. *Moral Issues and Christian Response*. Pt. 2. 3rd ed. New York: Holt, Rinehart & Winston, 1983.

Mace, David. *The Christian Response to the Sexual Revolution*. Nashville: Abingdon Press, 1970.

Mehl, Roger. *Society and Love: Ethical Problems of Family Life*. Translated by James Farley. Philadelphia: Westminster Press, 1964.

Nelson, James. *Embodiment: An Approach to Sexuality and Christian Theology*. Minneapolis: Augsburg, 1979.

Smedes, Lewis. *Sex for Christians: The Limits and Liberties of Sexual Living*. Grand Rapids, Mich.: Eerdmans, 1976.

7: Birthing and Dying

Callahan, Daniel. *Abortion: Law, Choice, and Morality*. New York: Macmillan, 1970.

Childress, James. *Priorities in Biomedical Ethics*. Philadelphia: Westminster Press, 1981.

Jersild, Paul and Dale Johnson, eds. *Moral Issues and Christian Response*. Chs. 14, 15. 3rd ed. New York: Holt, Rinehart & Winston, 1983.

Nelson, James B., and Jo Anne Smith Rohricht. *Human Medicine: Ethical Perspectives on Today's Medical Issues*. Chs. 2, 6, 7. Rev. ed. Minneapolis: Augsburg, 1984.

Ramsey, Paul. *The Patient as Person: Explorations in Medical Ethics*. New Haven: Yale University Press, 1970.

Shannon, Thomas, ed. *Bioethics: Basic Writings on the Key Ethical Questions That Surround the Major Modern Biological Possibilities and Problems*. Rev. ed. Ramsey, N.J.: Paulist Press, 1981.

Simmons, Paul. *Birth and Death: Bioethical Decision-Making*. Philadelphia: Westminster Press, 1983.

Smith, Harmon. *Ethics and the New Medicine*. Chs. 1, 4. Nashville: Abingdon Press, 1970.

8: Racial and Gender Relations

Allport, Gordon W. *The Nature of Prejudice*. Abr. ed. Garden City, N.Y.: Doubleday, 1958.

Cone, James. *God of the Oppressed*. New York: Seabury Press, 1975.

Daly, Mary. *Pure Lust: Elemental Feminist Philosophy*. Boston: Beacon Press, 1984.

―――. *The Church and the Second Sex*. Boston: Beacon Press, 1985.

Heyward, Carter. *Our Passion for Justice: Images of Power, Sexuality, and Liberations*. New York: Pilgrim Press, 1984.

Hough, Joseph C. *Black Power and White Protestants: A Christian Response to the New Negro Pluralism*. New York: Oxford University Press, 1968.

King, Martin Luther, Jr. *Strength to Love*. New York: Harper & Row, 1963.

―――. *Where Do We Go from Here: Chaos or Community?* New York: Harper & Row, 1967.

Lincoln, C. Eric. *Race, Religion, and the Continuing American Dilemma*. New York: Hill & Wang, 1984.

Russell, Letty. *Human Liberation in a Feminist Perspective: A Theology*. Philadelphia: Westminster Press, 1974.

9: Economic Ethics: Work and Vocation

Clark, Dennis. *Work and the Human Spirit*. New York: Sheed & Ward, 1967.

Forell, George, and William Lazareth, eds. *Work as Praise*. Philadelphia: Fortress Press, 1979.

Novak, Michael. *The Spirit of Democratic Capitalism*. New York: Simon & Schuster, 1982.

Raines, John, and Donna Day-Lower. *Modern Work and Human Meaning*. Philadelphia: Westminster Press, 1986.

Rasmussen, Larry. *Economic Anxiety and Christian Faith*. Minneapolis: Augsburg, 1981.

Schumacher, E. F. *Small Is Beautiful: Economics as if People Mattered*. New York: Harper & Row, 1973.

Shriver, Don, Jr. *Rich Man, Poor Man*. Richmond: John Knox Press, 1972.

Weber, Max. *The Protestant Ethic and the Spirit of Capitalism*. Translated by Talcott Parsons, 1920. Reprint. New York: Scribner, 1958.

Wogaman, Philip. *Economics and Ethics: A Christian Inquiry*. Philadelphia: Fortress Press, 1986.

10: Wasting and Wanting: The Ethics of Consumption

Abrecht, Paul, ed. *Faith, Science, and the Future*. Philadelphia: Fortress Press, 1979.

Birch, Bruce, and Larry Rasmussen. *The Predicament of the Prosperous*. Philadelphia: Westminster Press, 1978.

Center for Science in the Public Interest. *99 Ways to a Simple Lifestyle.* Garden City, N.Y.: Anchor Press, 1977.

Freudenberger, C. Dean, and Paul Minus. *Christian Responsibility in a Hungry World.* Nashville: Abingdon Press, 1976.

Hessel, Dieter T., ed. *Energy Ethics: A Christian Response.* New York: Friendship Press, 1979.

Shi, David E. *The Simple Life: Plain Living and High Thinking in American Culture.* New York: Oxford University Press, 1985.

Shinn, Roger Lincoln. *Forced Options: Social Decisions for the 21st Century.* San Francisco: Harper & Row, 1982.

Sider, Ronald. *Rich Christians in an Age of Hunger: A Biblical Study.* Downers Grove, Ill.: Intervarsity Press, 1977.

Simon, Arthur. *Bread for the World.* Rev. ed. New York: Paulist Press, 1984.

Taylor, John V. *Enough Is Enough: A Biblical Call for Moderation in a Consumer-Oriented Society.* Minneapolis: Augsburg, 1977.

11: Christian Ethics and Politics

Bennett, John. *Christians and the State.* New York: Scribner, 1958.

Berman, Harold J. *The Interaction of Law and Religion.* Nashville: Abingdon Press, 1974.

DeWolf, L. Harold. *Crime and Justice in America: A Paradox of Conscience.* New York: Harper & Row, 1975.

Míguez Bonino, José. *Toward a Christian Political Ethics.* Philadelphia: Fortress Press, 1983.

Neuhaus, Richard. *Christian Faith and Public Policy.* Minneapolis: Augsburg, 1977.

Niebuhr, Reinhold. *The Children of Light and the Children of Darkness.* New York: Scribner, 1944.

Richey, Russell, and Donald Jones, eds. *American Civil Religion.* New York: Harper & Row, 1974.

Stone, Ronald, ed. *Reformed Faith and Politics.* Washington, D.C.: University Press of America, 1983.

————. *Reinhold Niebuhr, Prophet to Politicians.* Nashville: Abingdon Press, 1971.

12: International Relations and the Nuclear Crisis

Bainton, Roland H. *Christian Attitudes toward War and Peace: A Historical Survey.* Nashville: Abingdon Press, 1960.

Bennett, John. *Foreign Policy in Christian Perspective.* New York: Scribner, 1966.

————, and Harvey Seifert. *U.S. Foreign Policy and Christian Ethics.* Philadelphia: Westminster Press, 1977.

Brown, Robert McAfee. *Making Peace in the Global Village.* Philadelphia: Westminster Press, 1981.

Geyer, Alan. *The Idea of Disarmament: Rethinking the Unthinkable.* Elgin, Ill.: Brethren Press, 1982.

Kennan, George. *The Nuclear Delusion: Soviet-American Relations in the Atomic Age.* Rev. ed. New York: Pantheon Press, 1983.

Ramsey, Paul. *War and the Christian Conscience: How Shall Modern War Be Conducted Justly?* Durham, N.C.: Duke University Press, 1961.

Union of Concerned Scientists. *Empty Promise: The Growing Case against Star Wars.* Edited by John Tirman. Boston: Beacon Press, 1986.

United Methodist Council of Bishops. *In Defense of Creation: The Nuclear Crisis and a Just Peace.* Nashville: Graded Press, 1986.

Yoder, John. *The Priestly Kingdom: Social Ethics as Gospel.* Notre Dame, Ind.: University of Notre Dame Press, 1986.

Index